S0-AAB-536

A PLUME BOOK

HOW TO GET DIVORCED BY 30

SASCHA ROTHCHILD grew up in Miami Beach, where she did stuff. She then went to college in Boston, where she learned stuff. Right after graduating with a concentration in playwriting, she moved to Los Angeles to begin her writing career and found there was a whole lot more stuff to do and learn. She lives there now with her cat.

HOW TO GET DIVORCED BY 30

My Misguided Attempt at a Starter Marriage

Sascha Rothchild

A PLUME BOOK

PLUME
Published by the Penguin Group
Penguin Group (USA) Inc., 375 Hudson Street, New York,
New York 10014, U.S.A.
Penguin Group (Canada), 90 Eglinton Avenue East, Suite 700, Toronto, Ontario, Canada
M4P 2Y3 (a division of Pearson Penguin Canada Inc.)
Penguin Books Ltd., 80 Strand, London WC2R 0RL, England
Penguin Ireland, 25 St. Stephen's Green, Dublin 2, Ireland
(a division of Penguin Books Ltd.)
Penguin Group (Australia), 250 Camberwell Road, Camberwell, Victoria 3124, Australia
(a division of Pearson Australia Group Pty. Ltd.)
Penguin Books India Pvt. Ltd., 11 Community Centre, Panchsheel Park,
New Delhi – 110 017, India
Penguin Group (NZ), 67 Apollo Drive, Rosedale, North Shore 0632,
New Zealand (a division of Pearson New Zealand Ltd.)
Penguin Books (South Africa) (Pty.) Ltd., 24 Sturdee Avenue, Rosebank, Johannesburg
2196, South Africa

Penguin Books Ltd., Registered Offices: 80 Strand, London WC2R 0RL, England

First published by Plume, a member of Penguin Group (USA) Inc.

First Printing, February 2010
1 3 5 7 9 10 8 6 4 2

 REGISTERED TRADEMARK—MARCA REGISTRADA

LIBRARY OF CONGRESS CATALOGING-IN-PUBLICATION DATA

Rothchild, Sascha.
How to get divorced by 30: my misguided attempt at a starter marriage /
Sascha Rothchild.
p. cm.
ISBN 978-0-452-29599-5 (pbk. : alk. paper) 1. Rothchild, Sascha. 2. Women
comedians—United States—Biography. 3. Marriage—Humor. 4. Marriage—
Anecdotes. 5. Man-woman relationships—Humor. I. Title.
PN2287.R764A3 2010
892.4'36—dc22   2009019802

Printed in the United States of America
Set in Sabon
Designed by Lenny Telesca

For Susan, who told me to write it down.
For John, who taught me how.

Contents

Contents

Contents

Acknowledgments

Although it was only me and my cat sitting at the computer days on end, it certainly takes a village to write a book. I am incredibly grateful to these invaluable people for helping me achieve this exciting, nerve-wracking, sometimes bizarre, and always insanely rewarding feat.

D. K., I will always cherish your support through thick and thin, literally.

Julie Engels, Craig Gerber, Mat Harawitz, Dave Nadelberg, Randi Barnes, Gabe Lewis, Allyson Rinella, Ben Blacker, Julie Lacouture, Lawrence McKibben, John Griffiths, Mike Ferrara, Buck Henry, Thomas Harris, and Jay Schuette, thanks for being fantastic friends who have listened to me, believed in me, bought me frozen yogurt in good times and bad, and read countless drafts of scripts, articles, pilots, pitches, and chapters.

Nate Hayden, without realizing it you got this ball rolling by strongly suggesting I send in writing samples to *LA*

Weekly when I was unemployed and panicking, and I am forever appreciative. *LA Weekly*, thank you for first publishing my article "How to Get Divorced by 30."

Chad Christopher, you are my entertainment lawyer extraordinaire, and I am lucky that you always have my back. Sarah Self, you are the best agent a writer could have and without your faith in me none of this would have happened. Thank you, thank you, thank you, Nadia Kashper, for being my phenomenal editor who truly gets me and knows how to make me better.

Chauncey, thanks for never treating me like a pesky little sister and for always being my wise loyal confidant. Berns, thank you for not only being my big sister but also being my best friend.

And Matt Kay, you changed my life by showing me not only is it okay to have feelings, but I can even safely reveal them and still be funny too.

HOW TO GET DIVORCED BY 30

Step 1

Don't Invite Your Husband to Your Thirtieth Birthday Party

"It's very sad when a five-year marriage only lasts two and a half years." "Do you have a quarter for the toll?"

Susan and John had unconventionally droll reactions when I told them I was getting a divorce. I guess my parents weren't surprised.

There had been major signs for months that I was unhappily married, and I'm not even talking about typical offenders like chronically passionless sex, crushes on coworkers, and the occasional fantasy my husband might die in a freak accident. Painlessly and quickly, of course. There were other, bigger signs. But it wasn't until talking to my sister, Berns, one day on the phone that I realized I wanted to end my marriage.

Berns is seven years older than me, half an inch shorter, and by far my favorite person in the whole wide world.

She has big lizard-green eyes, Shirley Temple ringlets, and heaps of compassion mixed in with the perfect amount of bitchiness. She will help a blind man cross the street while commenting on a passerby's tacky French pedicure. "Why would anyone want her toenails to look longer? Disgusting!" Berns can't walk a New York block without someone stopping her and asking, "Where did you get that?" And usually "that" is an item she herself made: a ruffled hat, a polka-dotted purse, a gold-plated chicken foot necklace. No matter how old I get, how many spats we have, or how much I might hate her clown chic taste, I can't seem to shake my big sister idolatry.

I was on the way to the gym when Berns called me from New York to discuss my upcoming thirtieth birthday. It was six months away, but with such a big milestone she wanted to start planning in advance. Did I want a huge party? Or a small dinner? Casual dress or cocktail attire? Costumes? A theme? Maybe I could finally get all my friends to dress goth. Who would I invite? Did I want to go somewhere? Vegas, like she did for her thirtieth? Back to Miami Beach, where we grew up? Or stay in Los Angeles, where I lived?

As we talked about the pros and cons of all these options, one definitive thought struck me: regardless of what city I was in or what I was wearing, I didn't want Jeff on the guest list. I didn't want Jeff to be anywhere near me on my thirtieth birthday. I wanted my thirtieth to be free of Jeff and all his status quo mediocrity.

This thought was both overwhelming and freeing and

struck me with such force I burst into tears. I should have been able to sob to Berns over the phone and explain what I was going through, but having been raised by a mother who wanted us to call her Susan—because "Mom" is so cliché—and who scorns any kind of raw emotion, crying was not something we did often, especially in front of each other.

"What? Berns, I can't hear you. Must be bad reception."

I quickly got off the phone and drove on, past actress-filled coffee shops, cell-phone-immersed dog walkers, and homeless men on roller skates, all blurred by my thick tears. Finally I arrived at the gym, pulled into the parking lot, and sobbed some more. I knew people were staring at me as they walked by my car but I didn't care. It was one of those rare and decadent moments when I really let it out. Snot and all.

When I was little and would cry, Susan would make me look at myself in the mirror. "See how puffy and silly you look? You don't want to look puffy, do you?"

After watching myself for a minute I would start to laugh. Because Susan was right: I did look puffy and silly. And pathetic. No mother, no matter how nonmaternal, wants to see her child crying. Susan couldn't handle my tears and thought she was being helpful by showing me how unattractive and unnecessary they were. It was better to hold them in and beat back all feelings with laughter, sarcasm, and cleverness. But the dam has to break some-times and when it does it's like a polluted river. All sorts

3

of things you didn't realize you were holding back come spilling out, and they are as toxic as mercury-filled fish carcasses, dirty needles, and used condoms.

The problem was, Jeff was my husband. And not wanting him to be with me on my thirtieth birthday was a feeling I couldn't ignore. In the scheme of relationship red flags, that one was crimson. After a few more minutes of parked car bawling, I looked at my face in the rearview mirror. I was already puffy and definitely pathetic. I pulled myself together and as I walked into the gym I knew I would be divorced by thirty.

Step 2

Date a Jerk in Your Early Twenties

About six years before my sobbing-in-the-car moment, I met Jeff at the comedy club the Improv, where we both worked. I was a struggling writer slash cocktail waitress. He was a struggling actor slash bartender. It was a romance made in L.A. heaven. I had broken up with my live-in boyfriend Adam only two months before Jeff and I had our first date. And like a game of Tetris, Adam's upside-down *L* shape turned and formed the space in my heart for Jeff's rectangle.

I met Adam in the beginning of my junior year of college. Susan's college friend Nancy, who she still kept in touch with, lived in Newton right next to the Boston College campus. When I arrived in Boston from Miami Beach, shocked by the icy cold winds, Catholics, and droves of pasty preppy students, I found comfort in Nancy's cozy, mezuzah-guarded brownstone. She took me out to dinner, drove me to run occasional errands, and let me do laundry at her place. I heard all about her four children; Adam, a doctor and expert on mandible reconstruction surgery, was one of them. My first two years of college he was busy with his residency and traveling the world helping children with cleft palates. Before that he had spent three years in Rwanda working in a clinic, so when I heard he was back in Boston and would be picking me up for Rosh Hashanah dinner, I was excited to finally meet the man behind the mandible.

As I walked outside my dorm I saw a cherry red 1968 Dodge Dart. I didn't know anything about old cars, or new cars for that matter, but I knew enough to know this car was supercool. I later learned that it was also completely impractical. It constantly broke down, was unbearably freezing as it had no working heat or insulation from the bitter Boston air, and with no power steering it was impossible to parallel park.

I saw two hands resting on the steering wheel. Even from my dorm steps, I could tell they were the most beautiful hands I had ever seen. No visible hair on the knuckles. Wide, masculine palms with long, perfectly proportioned fingers gently tapping on the wheel. The nail beds were large and clean and neat without looking manicured. The slightly raised veins stemming from the wrist conveyed a delicate strength. And to top it off, the muscle that rests between the base of the thumb and the forefinger was big and bulging.

People look at different things when they first meet a potential mate. Eyes. Lips. Bank accounts. I look at hands, always have. Big meaty paws are nice but it's not the size that's important, it's the proportion. The mix between grace and grab. Do I want those hands touching me? Do I want them gently caressing my hair, roughly pushing me against walls with wild abandon, and opening stubborn spaghetti sauce jars when I can't? That esoteric muscle, the one between the thumb and forefinger, the one that no one else seems to notice, is my favorite part of a man's body. It's all about grip strength, with some hand genetics thrown in. It is barely visible in women's hands, so to me, it defines masculinity. Baseball players, drummers, and bartenders always have the best hands. They're strong because they are constantly gripping bats, sticks, bottles, and breasts. Those three professions lend themselves to getting a lot of tail. After meeting Adam I added surgeons to that list. He had an extraordinary thumb muscle partly because he was always holding surgical tools with precision and control.

Once I got in the car, I saw that the rest of him didn't live up to his glorious hands. But because the hands were the first thing I saw and already made me want him, I was willing to overlook his Woody Allen nose, thinning hair, and small frame. He did have beautiful, mischievous blue eyes and a nice jaw, and all in all he was cute in a nebbishy way. And I was certainly in no position to only go for superhot guys. I had a horrible college haircut, I was a good fifteen pounds overweight, and I was struggling with my sense of style: at that moment it fell somewhere between goth light, club kid, desperate to be noticed, and disco.

As we dipped apple slices in honey and celebrated the Jewish New Year, it was clear Adam was extremely intelligent, sardonic, funny, passionate about his work, interesting, and in no way interested in me. He was ten years older, had traveled the world, spoke French, loved to rough it, and thought of me as a family friend. I thought of him as half of an amazingly romantic and fated love story about two kids ending up together forty years after their mothers were college chums.

The next time I saw Adam it was Passover and once again, he picked me up in his Dart for a Seder at Nancy's. We exchanged numbers that night and I didn't have to wait for Hanukkah to see him a third time.

Over the next year when he was in town and not saving sick people in third world countries, Adam and I often met up for dinner or a drink. We became friends and, because his residency was in a hospital forty-five minutes outside of Boston, he would sometimes crash in my bed after a night out. My crush on him grew, as did my confusion about why he didn't want to sleep with me. I was so focused on the fact that he *wasn't* interested, that I didn't think about why I *was* interested. One of the awesome side effects of being a nineteen-year-old girl.

Adam and I began spending more and more platonic time together and one weekend when Berns came to visit she met him and said, "He's one of us." I knew just what she meant. Not just that he was Jewish, but that he was quick, smart, sarcastic, and somewhat emotionally unavailable. The kind of guy who could pull out a biting and brilliant one-liner before anyone else. The kind of guy who was just like Susan.

One night during my senior year when we were out gallivanting (him driving my car because his was in the shop again), I decided to ask the question that had been irking me for so long.

"Why have we never fooled around?"

"Because you are ten years younger than me, a friend of my mom's, and now a friend of mine."

That night we had sex.

After two years of pining, it was amazing to feel his magnificent hands on my body. We cuddled all weekend, watching the December snow fall, and finally he got out of bed and left for South America on a three-month medical mission. Maybe it was so perfect because he was leaving. Maybe he let his guard down because he knew he was on his way out the door. Maybe that's why I let my guard down.

We left it casual and he said he would call. I didn't hear from him for weeks. In that time I convinced myself that he was a fucking asshole. I went on a few inconsequential dates and forced myself to find new crushes. In typical jerk fashion, Adam had warned me he might hurt me but I felt indestructible after my high school love, Billy, and I broke up. When Billy and I went to different colleges I thought I might die of a broken heart; and when I lived, I decided I would never be hurt again.

But when Adam didn't call, it hurt.

He finally did call, from a phone booth in some remote part of the world I couldn't locate in a hemisphere, let alone a country. The second I heard his voice I forgot that he was a fucking asshole. We talked a lot over the next couple of months and decided he would meet me in Miami Beach in March, when I would be home for spring break. Then we would drive back up to Boston together.

That week together in Miami Beach was all sunrises, sex, and the elation of a new relationship. Susan and John seemed to like Adam. Susan could practice her French and John could talk to him about their mutual passion for mountain climbing. And unlike all my previous boyfriends, Adam challenged me intellectually and wouldn't let me get away with dubious facts or undocumented quotes, like when I would say, "Did you know Tom Petty used to be a gravedigger?" or "I read that people who have a longer second toe than their big toe have royal blood," and "Against popular belief, the phrase 'look a gift horse in the mouth' did not come from the Trojan War." He called me out when I pretended to know more than I actually did, which was refreshing and sexy. I was used to being insecure about my appearance, but I never had doubts about my intelligence. So I was thrilled to have Adam give me a whole new arena of insecurity.

Adam watched foreign films, listened to jazz, and actually did good things for the world. I watched John Hughes movies, listened to the Cure, and occasionally would give homeless people my restaurant leftovers. Adam's confidence, compassion, and selflessness when it came to strangers in need blinded me to his arrogance. Instead of realizing he had good and bad points, I just allowed his good points to illuminate my bad ones. So he became perfect. And I became flawed. A dynamic he was all too happy to embrace.

During our road trip back to Boston, even though he controlled the radio like a music despot, corrected me constantly, and paid for nothing, I fell in love with him. Although he left for Morocco soon after we returned to Boston, I felt we might have a chance for a real relationship in the future.

A week after I graduated from Boston College, Phi Beta Kappa (take that, Adam), I moved to Los Angeles to pursue a writing career. I got an apartment, found a job cocktailing at a pool hall, and started writing. I also started dating. I didn't know where Adam would move once he finished his residency and I wasn't going to sit around and wait for him, especially since he often spoke about returning to Africa. For brief moments I felt my longing for him was so strong I would be willing to give up all my own plans and dreams and follow him to the Dark Continent. It would make for great material, and I would definitely lose weight. But then I thought about how much I love frozen yogurt, clean sheets, and the Internet and hate getting shots, getting dirty, and being depressed. If Adam and I were supposed to be together, he would have to come to me in Los Angeles.

Which he did. He came to visit for two weeks and we drove up the coast exploring everything California had to offer, from San Francisco sex shows to Hearst Castle's indoor pool to Venice Beach buskers. I was amazed at how Adam fit into each place with ease. I was used to dating guys who were only comfortable in their own environments, be it basketball courts, goth clubs, or bar mitzvahs. But Adam was versatile, capable, and knowledgeable enough to fit in anywhere. He seemed very much like a man. I guess at thirty-one he was a man and I probably shouldn't have been nearly as impressed as I was. But I was only twenty-one.

After his L.A. visit I went to Boston. We both stayed at Nancy's, where he was camped out until he decided where he was going to move permanently. While Adam was out one day with his buddies, I did a very bad thing. I looked through some of his papers that happened to be sitting on his desk. They weren't exactly hidden. But they weren't exactly out in the open either. I saw a few rough drafts of a letter he had written in English and was translating to French, a language commonly spoken in Rwanda. I knew right away that the letter was for Housna. I had heard her name countless times and knew all about her great beauty, grace, and strength. She was an African girl Adam had fallen in love with when he was there and they had a long and intense relationship. One the likes of which a very pale, spoiled Miami Beach girl couldn't possibly fathom. Housna was stuck in a country where women were mistreated, and not just those who were smart and educated and working toward reform. I couldn't compete with this girl and the mud hut pedestal Adam put her on, so I had to quietly listen to him talk about her. Which he did. Constantly.

My heart pounded as I riffled through those sheets of paper. I read the letter and with each word I became more and more nauseated. I had no right to read what wasn't meant for me but I couldn't stop. I was fully punished at the end of the letter when he claimed his undying and eternal love for her. And because she was a hostage in her own country and he was living it up in awesome America, I knew nothing would change his feelings. His memories would only get more intense.

Once the letters were placed back perfectly disheveled just where I found them, I tried to push that last line out of my mind. That night I did another bad thing.

"I love you," I said sternly as Adam was falling asleep.

The "love" word had been flapping around in my mouth for several months. I thought about it all those times I would lie awake hoping he would call me collect from some small, donkey-filled village. I thought about it while freezing in his Dodge Dart. And I thought about it in those moments when he would yell at me about something inconsequential and make my stomach drop.

"I told you not to touch the radio! I hate the perfume you're wearing! How can you not know the singular for lice is louse?"

I took the stomach drop to mean love instead of emotional abuse. So in that moment, perhaps to combat the love he felt for Housna, my love flew out of my mouth.

He did not say it back. He gave me a little squeeze and then fell asleep.

For anyone, saying "I love you" for the first time is nerve-wracking. Worse than being weighed in front of the whole class in PE, worse than having a cop behind you when you've had two drinks, worse than that moment when you realize you sent an e-mail about your boss to your boss instead of to your office buddy. And when the person says "I love you" back it's like realizing you don't weigh that much after all, that the cop is whizzing by you to pull over someone else, and by an act of God, the e-mail gets returned to you because your boss's e-mail box was full. But for me, coming from a family where no one ever said those three words, saying "I love you" was an even bigger deal. Not only did Susan never want to be called Mom, or any derivative of the word, she hated all clichés: I-love-yous, rainbows, teddy bears, and long hugs.

According to Susan, "I love you" is the biggest offender of all. It's overused and therefore diluted and meaningless. I'm sure my father would have said it and been thrilled to be called Dad, but with Susan running things of this nature, he was demoted to John. He had to lay his sentimental streak to rest when he met her. She scared it out of him. "I love you" was just never a part of the household vernacular. We were never taught to hear or say those words.

With the help of movies and TV shows and my friends' families, I learned all about the simple three-word expression. But because it sounded so foreign to me, I used it extremely sparingly and never to any of my family members for fear of being laughed at or scolded for my unoriginality.

When I was eighteen, while the whole family was together, I tried to hold an "I love you" intervention. We were in New York for the holidays and were gathered around in a friend's cozy living room playing hearts and watching the snow fall. Between the warmth of the fireplace, the comfy throw pillows, and just having shot the moon, I was overwhelmed with love. I wanted all of us to put the cards down, look each other in the eye, and say, "I love you."

It didn't go well.

To his credit, Chauncey really tried. He looked at me earnestly and said, "I—," and then he stopped. The rest of us couldn't even get the "I" out without sounding sarcastic. After a few tries we all burst into hysterics and laughed for hours.

My revelation to Adam was a huge leap. Him not saying it back felt like I was being drawn and quartered. The next morning he awkwardly drove me to Logan Airport in the Dart and I flew back home to L.A. with a team of imaginary masons reassembling my walls at an alarming rate.

That October he decided to move to L.A. The fact that he never said "I love you" loomed over me. He had the upper hand. But the fact that he chose to move into my apartment, over all the other places in the world, meant that I did have a certain amount of power. He planned to stay with me for a couple of weeks while he got his own place, but instead, he just stayed with me. And although the two of us had known each other for a few years, and been dating on and off for a year, we had never been in the same city for more than two months at a time. We had no business living together but it seemed convenient.

While he was studying for his California medical board exams, he wasn't making any money. So he also wasn't paying much rent. And as brave as I pretended to be, I was scared and lonely living in a new city all by myself. Manifest Destiny is overwhelming and a live-in boyfriend, even one who doesn't pay any of the bills and yells at you all the time, can take the edge off.

Looking back I see all of our relationship problems had already shown themselves. Adam was patronizing and mean and brought out the worst in me: defensiveness, combativeness, and insecurity. But the real trouble started when Adam officially moved in. He was messy and horribly unorganized and his things were piled all over my perfectly arranged, obsessively vacuumed apartment. He hated my purple color scheme, kitschy feather boas wrapped around everything, and ironic stuffed animals. Okay, maybe they weren't really ironic. But they were mine and I liked them sitting on top of my bookshelf watching over me.

Once he arrived he hounded me about my childish décor until I took everything that was *me* down. He also smoked tons of pot, which I hadn't noticed in Boston. To me, the difference between getting high on a Saturday night before a party and getting high every day before anything was the difference between letting loose and being a loser.

We fought constantly. Why was I so uptight? Why did I care that he had papers everywhere? Why did I mind that he had to get stoned before we went to a movie? Or went to dinner? Or went to breakfast? When he would hide behind a corner in the middle of a mall to take a hit off his little pipe I felt like I was back in high school. Actually, junior high, because by the time I was in high school, I had stopped hanging out with stoners.

But still, he was *my* stoner. And I loved him. He matched his every outburst of anger and hostility with kindness and tenderness. His dual personality (yes, he was a Gemini) kept me weathering the anger to get to the sweetness. At first his condescending antagonism was exciting and challenged me to become a well-rounded person: I read nonfiction, figured out where Rwanda was on a map, even went camping, hating every second of the fresh air, uncomfortable tent, and trail mix. But I pretended to love it.

As I mentioned earlier, Adam was a smaller guy. Five feet seven and skinny, weighing about 145 pounds. I was almost five feet six and certainly not fat, but not thin. By senior year of college I had dropped the freshman fifteen and was back down to a size 6, and when I moved to L.A. I was toned and firm and looked really good, but was still only ten pounds lighter than Adam. If we didn't fight constantly and sort of hate each other and we actually decided to get married, could he even carry me over the threshold? I doubted it. His size, and mine, made me feel like a big girl. And although many confident women on talk shows proudly extol their obesity, I didn't want to feel like a big girl.

In my first six months of L.A. life I worked out regularly and tried to keep up with the Hollywood standards. But when Adam moved in, and stocked the fridge with boy food, like tortilla chips and peanut butter, I slowly started gaining weight. He noticed. I certainly wouldn't expect him to be attracted to me if I completely let myself go and started wearing muumuus, but me gaining ten pounds didn't warrant constant berating. There needs to be a window of good days and bad. A window between fitting into your skinny jeans and buying one size bigger to get you through all those holiday parties.

One of Adam's favorite items was a green tea ice cream called Fubuki. It was so creamy and yummy, I couldn't resist grabbing a few spoonfuls throughout the day. He started calling me Fubuki Face. I told him that was very hurtful and to please stop. He told me it was a term of endearment. I told him I didn't feel endeared. He said he meant it in a cute way. I replied that it wasn't cute. He told me I had no sense of humor. So Fubuki Face continued.

I never confessed to Adam that I had read the letter. And whenever he mentioned Housna's most recent correspondence and her struggle to get out of Africa, I would grit my teeth and fear the day she would call him and tell him she was finally fleeing Rwanda and would be arriving on his doorstep. Our doorstep.

That New Year's Eve Adam told me he loved me. Three weeks later the call came in. We were both asleep when the phone rang at three thirty a.m. I knew the second I jolted up in bed that it was Housna, calling to ruin my already horrible relationship. She was escaping Africa and would arrive in Los Angeles in a few months. Adam told me in no uncertain terms she could either stay with us or he would move out and she could stay with him. I was furious he didn't even see how unreasonable he was being, asking his current girlfriend to house his ex-girlfriend who I knew he still loved because I'd read a letter I wasn't supposed to read. But he didn't see it as being unreasonable. He saw my hesitation at wanting her to move in with us as selfish, callous, and insanely unhumanitarian.

My "American home-of-the-free Jewish guilt" won out over my "it's insane to allow my boyfriend's ex to move into *my* apartment, regardless of her dire situation." Wasn't taking down all the purple things enough for him? Wasn't letting him keep piles of clothes in the corners proof that I was compromising? Now he was demanding I do this! But I relented and told him she could come. He assured me he no longer wanted to be with her but just wanted to help her. And although they would both be speaking French to each other, he would make sure to keep me included in all conversations so I wouldn't feel left out. Yeah, right.

By the time Housna called I had already stopped waitressing and landed an awesome job as the assistant to the executive producer of *The Late Late Show with Craig Kilborn*. So instead of freaking out about her imminent arrival, I channeled my Housna anxiety into my work. I made sure nothing was left in my in-box for more than five minutes. All calls were returned by the end of the day. I was a diligent and precise assistant. My phone had to be at a perfect ninety-degree angle on my desk, my purple pens had to be placed symmetrically on either side of my notepad, and no finger smudges were allowed on my shiny computer screen. My officemate, Owen, started to fuck with me by slightly moving things on my desk each time I left our office, just to watch me instinctively move the item back to its proper place. I realized that my OCD, which I always flirted with, was getting a little out of hand.

Instead of telling Adam to move out and live happily ever after with his true love, I went to therapy to deal with my increasing anxiety and need for perceived order. To punish Adam for his cruelty in not acknowledging my feelings, I started cheating on him with one of the writers on the TV show. During our premiere party I went to the bathroom and this funny, adorably disheveled, sexy cad, whom I playfully dubbed "the Devil," followed me into the bathroom, nudged me into a stall, and kissed me. Over the next few months he continued to kiss me, in his office, in a Banana Republic dressing room, under the desk in his office, in his apartment, in Vegas on a "work trip," and in many other torrid places.

Of course, I lied about all of this in therapy. I knew if I said I was cheating out loud, I would have no right to complain about Adam ever again. No matter how he treated me, I had no right to continually betray him. So I mentioned nothing in therapy but my unexplainable need to keep things perpendicular and symmetrical.

The meaner Adam became, the more I justified the cheating. The more he called me fat the more I wanted to feel attractive. And the Devil made me feel very attractive, always pulling me into inappropriate corners, making me believe I was so beguiling he couldn't wait one second longer to touch me. It never occurred to me to just break up with Adam and end the unpleasant and totally un-healthy cycle.

My initial admiration of his beautiful hands and his in-telligence turned into complete resentment and we couldn't get through a day without screaming at each other. It was so bad that I was embarrassed when passing by neighbors in the building because I knew they heard us yelling at each other all the time. Adam relentlessly nitpicked and cor-rected me. One of our worst fights started when we were at a Peruvian restaurant and a girl walked in wearing a purple pea coat.

"I like her pea coat," I said.

"Well, technically, it has to be navy blue to be a pea coat."

After months of gearing up for Housna's arrival, which consisted of Adam brushing up on his French and me having mild panic attacks, we heard news that she had successfully left Rwanda and, through a series of unforeseen events involving customs and airports and political asylum, she was safe and sound in Canada. Hooray! I was so relieved that I would never have to meet this woman, that I had shown I could be a good and caring person, willing to sacrifice my own happiness to help another truly in need. And so relieved it never came to that.

Adam and I continued to fight. I continued to cheat. I never had "actual" sex with the Devil. Like Bill Clinton, the no-intercourse policy was yet another way for me to justify something totally unjustifiable. Time passed with my usual brand of misguided acting out until the Devil completely double-crossed me by writing horrible things about me to a mutual acquaintance. I found out when he accidentally sent the e-mail to me. I was mortified. He wrote that I was "annoying and grasping" and how obnoxious I was for asking our friend if she could score me a T-shirt from her new job. He complained that I was always asking for things and I needed to give it a rest.

After reading the e-mail I was lonely, devastated, and inconsolable. Not that there would have been anyone to console me anyway. I think it's called karma and I didn't have a self-righteous leg to stand on. I had to cry about it alone. I still hadn't even told my therapist.

Because I still had to see the Devil every day at the show, and because I should have known that his devilish cruelty, which I was so intrigued by and attracted to in the first place, would eventually land on me, I forgave him and we settled into a cordial work relationship. My hostile romance with Adam continued on, as did my lifelong diary updates.

Instead of writing my usual daily recaps, my therapist advised me to write about my feelings. How did I feel about Adam?

He needs therapy. His cruel outbursts of pure anger directed at me need to end. He smokes pot, he leaves clothes around, he procrastinates, he is disliked by many of my friends, and he is stubborn, condescending, and tactless. But his hands, his beautiful hands. But that's not a feeling. How do I feel? Obviously Adam doesn't give me what I need or I wouldn't have been roaming around with the Devil. But that's not a feeling either. How do I feel? I just saw a crippled baby elephant on the Discovery Channel. I cried. It was horrible to watch the poor little thing try to walk. But he made it. The little guy picked himself up and made it. Just goes to show a little determination . . . But how do I feel? Definitely confused.

A few months later, after having to wear a bikini in front of Adam on what should have been a romantic getaway to Kauai, I joined a gym and met Mary, a personal trainer who became a close friend. With her help, my resolve, and my vitriol toward Adam egging me on, I lost thirty pounds. Call me Fubuki Face now, fucker! That September I broke up with him. He might say he broke up with me. Regardless, we broke up and he moved out.

Because we were so codependent and not ready to cut all ties, and he was still my cat Spork's pseudo vet, we continued to spend time together even after he moved out, and just said our relationship was downsizing.

Me and my new size 2 body started dating immediately. And although I loved my assistant job, I had been there over a year and I had learned all I could in that position. It was time to quit and again focus on my writing.

So to pay the bills, I got a part-time job cocktailing at the Hollywood Improv. That's where I met Jeff.

Step 3

Don't Give Yourself a Minute to Reflect

I don't remember the first time I saw Jeff. I don't even remember the first time I spoke to him. I was too busy being single, self-absorbed, and skinny. And because I was the new girl at the illustrious comedy club the World Famous Improv, I was the new conquest for all the comics. I lapped up the attention with the grace of a drunk warthog. I wore sheer skintight tops with no bra to show off my toned body and perky boobs. I wore tons of eyeliner to let people know I was a badass. I was like a starving caged lion just let out into a room full of injured wildebeests; not sure which to eat first, I haphazardly flirted with everyone, including the other female servers.

One after the other, I dated three guys. Cody, an incredibly hot, leather-jacket-wearing, non-hair-washing, brilliantly funny bad-boy comic I met at the Improv; Sam, a tall, handsome, successful Australian director with some mysterious undertones, whom I met at a party; and Alex, a sexy, long-blond-haired, perfect-six-packed, once marginally successful rocker still clinging to the dream, whom I met at dinner with friends.

After my shift, I would hop into the bathroom, change out of my Improv babydoll T-shirt and black pants, and put on my date clothes, which often consisted of, but were not limited to, sequins, pleather, and mesh. Growing up in Miami Beach, surrounded by feather-bound drag queens, neon-covered buildings, and rhinestone-encrusted bikinis, had had an effect on me. I loved all of it and although I knew enough about good taste to always pretend my tackiness was really kitschiness, it wasn't. It was just plain tackiness. The walk from the Improv bathroom, across the club, to my car was always a fun burst of attention. All eyes were on me, the guys staring at my outrageous skin-baring attire, the girls rolling their eyes at my clear desperation. Jeff was the one person who never seemed to notice one way or the other.

Cody and I went out several times. He drank red wine and wore just a touch of black eyeliner. He was edgy and clever and when I watched his stand-up my stage lust grew stronger. Stage lust is the age-old feeling of being attracted to whoever is onstage, whether it is a musician, an actor, or even a surgeon being watched from the observation deck. Someone you might not notice if they were just walking down the street becomes a sex symbol because he is good enough at what he does to be watched by others. And being good at something is the sexiest thing of all.

Cody was the first, and only, comic I slept with, and he told all the others immediately. Instead of feeling cheap and used, I was thrilled to be considered hot enough to brag about banging. But as I walked through the Improv the next night, seeing the guys give him the nod, and seeing him give me a wink, I wanted details of exactly what he was saying. Was he saying I rocked his world? Was he saying I was the coolest chick ever? Or was he saying I was annoying and grasping? I wanted to know what Cody was saying but to get a real answer I had to ask someone neutral. I assumed the other waitresses would be jealous and the other comics would be secretive so I needed to ask someone who didn't seem to be involved in the silliness of my life. Someone like Jeff.

Although he barely said one word to me, I became aware that every Sunday, when the new week's employee schedule went up in the back office, I would check to see when Jeff was working. He wasn't particularly handsome, he was definitely dorky, with a bad haircut and an even worse style of glasses, and he was kind of fat. But for some inexplicable reason, when he was around I felt a calm pass over my usually frantic soul.

Jeff was standing outside rolling a cigarette and I bounced right up to him to get some information.

"Based on what Cody is saying about me, do you want to sleep with me more, or less?"

27

Jeff looked down at me, cigarette now perfectly cylindrical. "What makes you think I want to sleep with you at all?"

He knocked the newly skinny, overly cocky self-assuredness right out of me. How could the dork not want to sleep with me at all? I dress like a slut, I have flat abs, and I'm full of moxie. A bit stunned, I backed away from him into the safety of the crowded club.

Cody and I continued to date for a few weeks, until I heard a distinctive clink when he was using my bathroom. It was the clink of my migraine pills against the side of their plastic container. I had suffered from severe migraines since I was sixteen, and after many failed attempts to keep them at bay with Imitrex, Susan gave me a Fioricet. She had them to help with her headaches and, amazingly, they worked for my migraines. I have had a prescription ever since, and although they can bring on a nice dazed, buzzed feeling I never abused them. They were for the unbearable pain of my migraines and only for the unbearable pain of my migraines.

When Cody walked out of my bathroom I was standing right in front of the door and without warning I shoved my hands into his pockets. I felt a handful of pills and dragged them out of his tight pants. I screamed and yelled, "This isn't some fun drug! How could you steal from me? Get out!"

The next night at the Improv he was onstage doing a comedy bit about how a great way to fuck up a good thing with a girl is to get caught stealing her migraine pills. The audience laughed. I didn't. A friend of mine from college who also happened to work at the Improv watched the bit and chuckled. He found me in the back bar grabbing my tray of drinks and said, "Didn't you know Cody was a drug addict? He'll take anything. Everyone here knows that."

Now *I* knew.

After everyone in the club heard about my breakup with Cody, Jeff started acknowledging me a bit more. As I walked by him in my porn star outfits he would just shake his head and say, "Cover those things up." One night he actually threw his jacket over me. I guess, against his better judgment, he couldn't help but feel a bit protective over me.

Then there was Sam. I had been out on three dates with Sam when he invited me to a Halloween party in Hollywood. As always, I was a vampire. I had a lifelong recurring propensity for goth, so I had a variety of vampire costumes and custom-made fangs at my disposal. I wore a sheer black spiderweb dress, five-inch black heels, and my longest fangs. I had just applied my final coat of bloodred lipstick when Sam knocked on the door. He was wearing a standard striped prisoner costume and he looked adorable.

We danced, we drank, and we stood around trying not to stare at all the really famous people we didn't know. He kissed me in dark corners and I nibbled on his neck with my fangs.

Just after midnight we spilled into my apartment and

made our way to the bedroom. Until this point we had only kissed, and it was clear by the way we were ripping the costumes off each other that we weren't stopping there tonight. We started fooling around and, like a gentleman, Sam got me off first. It was then that I noticed he wasn't hard at all. No matter what I was doing to him, he wasn't getting hard. Of course my first thought was, *I look fat in my costume. And I look fat now that I'm naked. And he thinks I'm fat.* And then I went over the speech in my head. The "it's not about me" speech. *I'm not fat. Maybe he drank too much. Maybe he's nervous. Maybe he's preoccupied. Maybe he's gay. It's not me; it's him.*

Sam was seemingly unfazed by his nonerection so I gave up trying to get him hard. He asked me if I had my high school yearbook.

"Yes, I do."

"Will you go get it?"

"Um, sure. What year?"

"Senior year. Definitely senior year."

I got out of bed and walked to the bookshelf, still naked. I grabbed my yearbook and brought it back to the bed. Maybe he wants to reminisce, I thought. Maybe he knows someone who went to my high school. Maybe he just wants to change the topic since he clearly isn't going to get hard. I had no idea what was going to happen next but in the back of my mind I thought, if nothing else, this was going to make for a great story.

I lay there in as sexy a position as possible and handed him my yearbook. He flipped through the pages until he found me. There I was, smiling. With all my clubs and accomplishments listed next to my picture: Drama Club, Advanced Placement classes, Octagon, Student Council, Honor Society.

Then he started jerking off. I was too shocked to react. I wasn't offended or outraged, just totally confused. Here was my date, dick now hard, jerking off to a picture of me in my senior yearbook, while I was lying in front of him *naked*!

It wasn't until he actually came and got some on the page that I was annoyed.

I walked him to the door.

"Hey, tonight was really great. Do you want to meet for breakfast tomorrow morning?"

"No, thanks," I said and left it at that. I like to think of myself as pretty open-minded and not easily rattled, but that was one weird fetish I had never heard of. At least he didn't try to steal my migraine pills.

The third guy I dated was Alex. He was a friend of my best friend Jennifer's boyfriend. I met him one night at a dinner party and then reported back to Jennifer that I thought he was cute. She reported back to her boyfriend that he thought I was cute. Thus our relationship began. I read in some magazine years ago that there are three elements needed for a good relationship. The gist, as I understood it, was . . .

1. The person has to make you feel the way you want to feel in public.
2. The person has to make you feel the way you want to feel in private.
3. The person needs to make you feel like a man, or woman, whatever that means to you.

I always thought about those three things and am aware when one or two or all three are lacking. Adam was amusing and successful and interesting so in public he came across as a pretty great catch. In private he was mean and hostile. Because he was small, and I felt he couldn't throw me over his shoulder and carry me out of a burning building, he didn't make me feel particularly feminine. He had one out of the three.

Alex had two out of three. In my tacky, delusional mind, we looked great together. I loved walking into bars and clubs and restaurants with him, publicly doubling my awesome image. We both had long, thick, wavy hair, his blond, mine strawberry. We both wore skintight leather pants and had cool silver rings. When he kissed me, his six-foot, 185-pound frame easily picked me up and twirled me around. When his rolling desk chair accidentally went over my foot and crushed my toe, he scooped me up in his arms and dramatically walked me over to the bed, gently placing me down like the toned rocker-goth princess that I wanted to be. I felt like such a girl with him, in a really good way. He always paid, opened car doors for me, and made sure I wasn't getting mauled at concerts. The element we lacked was how I felt with him in private. He was a good guy, but we didn't have much to talk about. He was New Age. I was old cynical. He used words like "vibe" and "energy" and "aura" and I used words like "whatever." And although Alex was totally hot, when it came down to it there wasn't much of a connection between us sexually so we never consummated the relationship.

Once Adam moved out and I started the Cody, Sam, Alex succession, I didn't give myself one second to reflect on our three-year relationship. I didn't take the time to learn anything about who I was now. I didn't ask myself why I had fallen in love with Adam in the first place, why it fell apart, why I cheated, and what should be different next time. I was still spending time with Adam while I was dating these new guys, which confused the issue even more. I wasn't able to cut all ties, so the knot just got more tangled.

All the while I would study Jeff from afar. He had an inner confidence and calm that needed no contrived clothes or accoutrements. He wore the same thing every night: an old ratty trench coat, ill-fitting faded jeans, black sneakers, and the required black Improv T-shirt. His hands were broad, with wide palms and short meaty fingers. Not nearly as beautiful as Adam's, but they were dexterous and capable. I was mesmerized when watching Jeff roll his own cigarettes and cut dozens of lemons and limes before his shift.

Night after night I studied him as he made apple martinis, stacked his glassware, idly and easily chatted with patrons from small-town tourists to studio presidents, appeased insecure comics, defused angry drunks, and took cigarette breaks. Lots of cigarette breaks, where he would stand outside, trench coat slightly fluttering around his large frame, thick hands delicately sprinkling tobacco on the square paper, tongue casually licking the edge after it was rolled. I realized that, with a little help, he had a lot of potential. I didn't want to date him, but I wanted to be near him. I wanted him to be my friend. And my project.

One night in early November, I stormed up to him and said, "You know, you would be cute with new glasses."

"Yeah, okay. It's probably time anyway. Want to help me pick them out?"

"Yes. When?"

"Thursday."

"Okay."

And I bounced back into the club.

That Thursday, while putting dozens of glasses on Jeff's face and saying yes or no, I learned he was from Chicago, half Jewish, and an actor. His sense of humor came from the Jewish part, his warmth from the Chicago part, and his effortless charisma from the actor part. I got rid of the giant round metal frames he had had since Windows 3.1, *Sister Act,* and Boyz II Men were just coming out, and picked out square plastic frames, which offset his round face and gave him a hipster nerd look. He purchased two pairs.

Step 4

Arrive with the Old, Leave with the New (in the Same Night)

Over the next week Jeff and I spent a lot of time together. He knew I had just ended a long relationship, that I had slept with Cody, and that I was dating other guys. There was something so liberating in not having to lie to him about anything or anyone. Cheating on Adam and keeping it a secret for so long was exhausting, draining, and a waste of everyone's time. I vowed if I started a new relationship to be honest and up-front about everything, and never to read private letters that happen to be sort of sitting out, again.

Jeff's glasses arrived. He put them on and he was adorable. That night we hung out in Venice, had dinner, took a long walk on the beach, and went back to his apartment. He put on a Ween album and casually noted, "This is my favorite song." I listened. I wanted to know every word and hear every note of Jeff's favorite song. Maybe within that song I would somehow unlock his indescribable coolness. We sat silently for the eight-minute song and he would later tell me that was the moment he knew I was a good egg. He knew if I could sit quietly for an entire song that I had more depth than my façade revealed.

By two a.m. I was too tired for the thirty-minute drive home to Hollywood. I crashed in his bed and immediately fell sound asleep. He woke me up and said, "I really want to kiss you." I thought, why not? If I really just wanted to be friends I wouldn't be in his bed wearing tiny boy shorts with little balloons all over them, I wouldn't be glancing at his work schedule so I could try to have the same shifts, and I definitely wouldn't be driving all the way to Venice for no other reason than to see him.

Susan will have to excuse me for using such a terrible cliché, but that first kiss was like fireworks going off in my entire body. I felt it everywhere, especially in my heart, which I had given up on. We kissed for hours, until my mouth hurt, and then I cuddled up into his big teddy bear chest and slept.

On November fifteenth of that year I celebrated my twenty-fourth birthday. I planned a party at the hipster Standard Hotel in Hollywood, which is known for its bowls of Jolly Ranchers and condoms, futuristic white bubble chairs, and glass tank with a hot chick inside looking out at the world with a stare of complete boredom. The plan was dinner there with a few close friends, then drinks at the bar with a big group.

Even though I knew it was wrong, I continued to hang out with Adam because it felt so familiar. Since Jeff couldn't make it to my gathering because he had to work, and Adam felt strongly about spending my birthday with me, I invited him. Adam insisted on driving me to the dinner.

"No, that's okay. I'll drive myself and just meet you there."

"Let me drive you."

"No, thanks, really. I'll see you there."

"Stop being so difficult. I'll drive you. What's the big deal?"

"Fine. Come pick me up at seven thirty."

"Oh, well, why don't you take a cab to my house and then we can drive from here?"

I didn't want to take a cab to his house. I didn't even want to see him at all. I knew this whole "let me drive you, but I'm not picking you up so take a cab" routine was yet another subtle power play and when I got angry and accused him of being manipulative he told me I was "way too sensitive and paranoid."

I wore skintight black pants, an off-the-shoulder black top that showed off my collarbones, and intimidating black boots. I got out of the cab in front of Adam's house and as he hugged me hello, he actually told me I was too skinny. I relished every second of his concern.

I drank and chatted and basked in my twenty-four-year-old wisdom. I stared at the hot chick in the tank, then tried to not stare, then stared some more and vowed to one day be the chick in the tank. Special enough to be put on display, cool enough to seem bored by it all. Then I saw Jeff walk in, trench coat billowing over his Improv T-shirt. My heart, the one I recently discovered I still had, leaped. I introduced him to everyone, Adam included.

As the night came to a close we all walked out to the valet. Adam assumed that I would be leaving with him. But now was my moment to make a definitive stand. So when Jeff offered me a ride home, I told Adam I was leaving with Jeff. Adam stood there, staring at me, a bit stunned. I felt bad for a second but I quickly pushed my pity away. Before Adam got inside his Dart he looked at Jeff, raised his hands in the air, and said, "Good luck, man."

If I was really cool and it was the end of a coming-of-age movie, I would have told both guys I needed to be alone. I would have ended things for good with Adam and told Jeff I wasn't ready to begin anything new and both would have stood together and watched me as I walked down Sunset Boulevard alone, with the self-assuredness of someone who knows that with solitude comes maturity and growth. Instead, I hopped in Jeff's car excited to punish Adam one last time and rushed right into a new relationship with a whole new set of problems.

Step 5

Marry a Big Guy Just So You Feel Small

I had never dated a guy who was overweight before. They had all either been skinny or in superb muscular shape. Either way, I always felt insecure about my own body. Jeff was five feet ten, a respectable height for a half-Jewish guy, and weighed about 210 pounds, most of it in his broad shoulders and big belly. He wasn't stare-at-that-gross-guy-in-line-at-Disney-World fat. He was adorable-sitcom-husband-teddy-bear fat. And when I was in his arms, I felt tiny.

My lifelong fat complex went from mild to severe when I was nine years old and a kid tried to say my name and it came out sounding sort of like "sausage." Another kid caught that immediately and started in.

"Sausage, sausage!"

"Ugly sausage!"

"Big ugly sausage!"

"Big fat ugly sausage!"

It's difficult for kids to stay interested in anything for more than five minutes but somehow torturing me occupied this group for hours. And this was 1985, before the surge in popularity of Ritalin.

Big Fat Ugly Sausage became my nickname. And what bothered me almost as much as the sentiment was how redundant and uncreative it was. Why did they have to include big *and* fat? Fat ugly sausage would have been enough. Sausages are already ugly, so did they really need all those adjectives? Big and ugly. Big and fat and ugly. Fat ugly sausage. Big ugly sausage. I guess "big fat ugly sausage" is better for chanting.

Hell is different things to different people. To me, hell is being stuck on a dolphin-watching boat with a battalion of evil nine-year-olds chanting "Big fat ugly sausage" over and over and over again. The boat ride lasted for three hours, but the chanting was eternal.

I wasn't fat, by any standards. A tad chubby, maybe. I had round cheeks. But I wasn't fat. I fit into children's clothing, I always passed the Presidential Fitness Test, and I could easily see my feet. The most ironic thing is that one of the ringleaders that day was a boy named Chris. He was two years older than me and really was fat, plus-size-Old-Navy fat. How could the kids call me fat when someone so much fatter was sitting next to me? The injustice was mind-boggling.

Aside from a lifetime complex about being fat, that

day also gave me a great disdain for dolphins. As I watched them play alongside the boat while I was being berated it seemed like they were siding with my attackers. Instead of coming to my aid, the second smartest mammals on Earth were joining in the fun and mocking me.

I hated being nine years old. I hated that on a whim, a few months earlier, I had shaved my head at horseback-riding camp with grooming shears and now looked like a boy. I hated Sea Camp, which was three days of basic aquatic lessons held in Key West. I felt icky surrounded by the urchins, the sea cucumbers, the kelp, and most of all, the other kids. All the girls were named Christy and Kristen and Crissy and they had perfect long blond French braids, lots of inside jokes, and no sense of irony.

I was in fourth grade and everyone on this three-day Sea Camp excursion went to my elementary school. It was my first year at the small private school and the rest of the kids had known each other since kindergarten, which made me the weird new kid. It didn't help that my name wasn't derived from the New Testament, I had boy hair, and I sometimes ate tempeh for lunch since I was on a vegetarian kick. Being new when you're an awkward pre-teen isn't nearly as fun as being new when you're a cute cocktail waitress.

Unfortunately for me Sausage had staying power and once Sea Camp was over and we all returned to the routine of school, it wasn't long before some of my teachers adopted my new moniker. They had the nerve to call me Sausage in front of my peers.

"Sausage, please come to the board and finish this problem."

"Sausage, excellent report on Margaret Mead."

"Sausage, you know black nail polish is not acceptable at this school."

To be fair, once you start hearing Sausage instead of Sascha, it's easy to slip up. Soon it becomes a habit. I know because I had a similar experience that year. I listened to Dr. Ruth on the radio every night before bedtime so the word "orgasm" was constantly skipping around in my head. When it came time to study organisms in fourth grade science class I accidentally called them orgasms during my oral report. And once the wrong word flew out of my mouth, I kept saying it and couldn't stop. Fully aware of what an orgasm was, I was embarrassed. In conjunction with Dr. Ruth's explanation, Susan told me it was "a nice feeling you can give to yourself, or someone else can give you, usually with a hand, mouth, or penis." Every time I said "orgasm" the science teacher was mortified. But none of the other kids reacted. I guess their parents didn't allow them to listen to Dr. Ruth.

But there is still no excuse for Sausage. The kids were cruel but the teachers were just too lazy to say my name correctly. I had to remind myself that one day I would be incredibly thin and beautiful and successful and those teachers would still be explaining basic math to snotty kids and drinking bad coffee in the lounge.

I'm not sure what became of any of those teachers. I

do know what became of me, however. I drink very good coffee every morning.

At the time of the Sea Camp trauma, I was four feet ten and weighed ninety pounds. According to a few charts I thoroughly studied when at the doctor's office, I was technically five pounds overweight. That five pounds haunted me like a phantom double chin.

I know my exact weight at nine years old, because I kept thorough records of it in my diary. I have kept thorough records of everything. I would shuffle into the breakfast room where Susan and John would be competing to see who could finish *The New York Times* crossword puzzle first—they both had their own copy—and I would start telling some story about seeing the smallest man in the world at school because he was this girl's uncle, and she was holding him in one arm and I thought he was a monkey until he started speaking Spanish, and I thought, *That's one smart monkey!* Or about one of our five cats, Snuffy, Fluffy, Noodle, Strudel, and Picky. Or I would tell about my recurring anxiety dreams in which I was being held down while salt was shoved into my mouth. No matter what I told them (all things true, by the way), Susan would respond the same way.

"Write it down."

"Are you writing it down?"

"You should really be writing this stuff down."

I grew up watching John sit in his office hours on end writing it down. Like observing an animal at the zoo, I would peer at John through the glass door of his long, thin office and I learned writing is one percent inspiration and ninety-nine percent playing solitaire on the computer. But seeing him sitting there day after day, year after year, knowing that whatever he was typing would soon be in bookstores or on magazine stands read by complete strangers seemed very fulfilling. So I listened when Susan told me to "write it down." Half my life I lived; the other half I wrote it all down.

By the time I was in fourth grade my diary had heard a lot about my dieting. I constantly weighed myself on the big fancy doctor's scale that lived in Susan's walk-in closet. My safe haven from the fat jokes at school should have been at home where my parents would smother me with kisses and positive reinforcement. That didn't happen. Susan was just as much to blame for my fat complex as the kids on the boat. But at least she didn't call me Sausage.

She called me Snausage.

This was during the Snausages dog treat commercial era, where the cute dog would run around the house demanding snausages. Being called Snausage was somehow less offensive than Sausage but still not ideal, especially since it was coming from my mother.

Susan also called me her "little hippo baby." When I protested she would remind me, "Hippopotamus babies are the cutest!" But last I checked, and I often did by watching hippo footage on nature shows, no little girl wants to look like one.

Susan and I passed a Carvel ice cream shop five days a week on the drive home from my prissy, plaid-uniform-laden elementary school. We also passed lots of hookers hanging out on Biscayne Boulevard. Like the punch buggy game most kids play when in the car, I played spot the hooker. That was one of the great things about Miami in the eighties—mansions and crack dealers were just blocks apart. My little school, filled with uptight behavioral codes, was surrounded by hookers. And I was enamored with them. I was fascinated by their scuffed heels, teased hair, and neon miniskirts, and with the notion that they were so beguiling, men would pay to have sex with them. And they weren't all skinny. Actually, most of them were plump if not straight-up fat. Thighs overlapping and rubbing together. Boobs spilling out over their untoned abs. They clearly were allowed to eat whatever they wanted, including ice cream, and they still got to charge men for sex.

"Susan, can we stop at Carvel?"

"I thought you were on a diet."

"I am. But I just want a treat this one time."

"It's your choice. But just remember thin tastes better than ice cream."

I heard this all the time. Thin tastes better than Pudding Pops, pasta, key lime pie, carrot cake, peanut butter cookies, and chocolate. For someone who hates clichés so much, Susan certainly had no problem abusing this axiom.

I found later she wasn't wrong. Now thin *does* taste better than ice cream but thin takes years of work and ice cream is right now. Susan would never admit that her dogmatic approach to my eating yummy treats stemmed from her own inability to curb her frantic cookie desires. I found empty sleeves of Vienna Fingers crammed behind her Volvo seats on more than one occasion. Instead of warning me that a lack of self-discipline runs in the family, she tried to prevent me from ever tasting sugar at all. Her plan worked for the first two years of my life.

I was born November 15, 1976, at 12:45 p.m. in a Naples, Florida, hospital, a Scorpio. Through no fault of my own, I started out huge and weighed a whopping ten pounds. Aside from being off-the-baby-charts heavy, I was in perfect health. From the moment I popped out I looked exactly like John. I still do. Big blue wide-set eyes that mask nothing, a small button nose, and nonexistent cheekbones. I looked so much like him that the joke at the hospital was "Who's the mother?"

At the time of my birth, Susan was a thirty-eight-year-old socialite hippie New Yorker, John was a thirty-one-year-old middle-class Yalie journalist, and they weren't married. Both of them had already dropped out of society and moved to the nonexistent swamp town of Everglades City. They had been traveling around the country from commune to commune writing the book *Children of the Counterculture* and the Everglades was the last stop. They decided to stay.

I guess Naples was the closest place with an actual working hospital. The only thing the Everglades had was alligators, mosquitoes, key lime trees, and drug dealers.

46

We lived in a half-completed wooden house on stilts that John built. Not much else was around except for a few other houses on stilts and some scattered trailers. My parents got married that New Year's Eve at the tiny courthouse. They claim they had nothing else to do that night. I was six weeks old at their wedding and wore red. Chauncey was nine and Berns was seven. My siblings' biological father had died of lung cancer five years prior, leaving Susan a widow.

For the first couple years of my life all I ate was homemade hippie chemical-free mashed-up bananas and peas—nothing processed, no sugar, no canned baby food. But Susan could shield me from sugar for only so long. The minute I started preschool, and got out into the world and met Pumpkin, there was no going back. Pumpkin lived in a trailer near our house. She sat on the trailer steps, rolls of fat bursting out of her pink shorts and matching tank top, and ate candy for breakfast. She didn't like the taste of water so she only drank soda. By three years old she had rotten baby teeth. She was my best friend. It was with her that I first discovered Veryfine fruit punch. I also discovered that my key to getting sugary food items would be my friends.

When I was three years old I had to say good-bye to Pumpkin. John had written an article for *Rolling Stone* magazine about all the drug dealers in the Everglades quietly smuggling pounds of God knows what into Florida through the forgotten swamps. The dealers didn't take kindly to being exposed and it was clearly time to leave.

We left the muggy mosquito-infested bogs and moved to pastel pink and ocean-bound Miami Beach.

Because we never had junk food in the house (Susan secretly ate hers in the car) I always went bonkers when it was around. It was my first glimpse into the world of addiction, and I continued to choose friends based on their kitchen loot.

Sharon, a girl I was never all that fond of, had the best snacks—Pop-Tarts, Twix, gummy bears, and Soft Batch cookies. And she was so skinny! Probably because the yummy goodness was always around she didn't feel the need to ravenously shovel it into her face. I never knew where my next fix would come from, so whenever I had the chance, I had to binge. I would shove a cold Pop-Tart into my mouth while waiting for the second one to toast.

One day a can of SpaghettiOs accidentally made it into our grocery bag and ended up on our kitchen counter. I felt it was serendipitous and it would be a shame to let it go to waste, so without consulting Susan I heated it up and put it in a bowl. That same day our house was broken into and Chauncey's stereo was stolen. Police officers came over to take a report and there I was eating SpaghettiOs. I felt so normal. A normal kid who was eating normal kid food, and I even had cops as my witnesses.

Growing up, my entire fantasy life was mostly built around being skinny. Although I never believed in God, I did pray every night . . . to demons. I even made up a poem when I was seven years old:

Demons demons of the night
Upon my life please shine some light
And make me skinny, alright?

The demons took care of the day-to-day realistic wants. I want a gold star in class for having the best essay. I want to win my tennis match so John will love me. I want kittens.

When it came time for more fanciful magical wishes, I prayed to genies. I want to be kidnapped by pirates. I want to be beautiful. I want to be a vampire. I want to be kidnapped by beautiful vampires.

My first wish to the genies was consistently the same. I wished that every time I ate a gummy bear I would lose a pound. I knew genies could be wily so I was very specific so as not to get tricked:

1. I want to lose a pound of fat, not muscle or bone or brain matter.
2. I want that pound to melt off in a proportionate way, so as not to have one very skinny leg and one normal one.
3. I want the magic removal of the pound of fat to be seamless and painless.

Even after covering all my bases and establishing the rules and guidelines to this wish, I feared if it did somehow come true, tragic irony would take hold and gummy bears would stop being produced. So then I would imagine having to go to Costco and buying up as many giant bags of gummy bears as possible and storing them in a trunk in my closet with all my diaries, telling no one.

My other wishes have changed over the years depending on my station in life. I wished to get a 1400 on my SATs. I wished to get into Yale. I wished to sell a movie script. But to this day the gummy bear wish remains. I realize now that if the Devil exists (not the one I cheated on Adam with but the real one), I would've sold my soul by the time I was in second grade.

A lifetime of gummy bear wishes is why I felt so content about myself when I was with Jeff. He made me feel skinny not only because of his size, but because he never judged my body. He never gave me a sideways glance when I wanted to order dessert. He never nudged me to do more cardio. He never looked at me for a second too long while I was getting out of the shower (and I can tell the difference between a "you look hot when you're wet" look and a "wow, you would be hotter if you were ten pounds thinner" look). When we first started dating, Jeff would give me bouquets of sour apple Blow Pops. He would bring me carrot cake from the Improv at the end of his shift and we would eat it in bed together at two a.m. while reciting hackneyed comedy bits we had heard for the eightieth time that night. We would laugh hysterically until we started choking on the cloyingly thick cream cheese frosting. Jeff introduced me to warm glazed donuts. He silently gave me permission to be fat.

And so by the second year of our relationship I had

gained that thirty pounds back. I couldn't have maintained that low, recently single weight anyway. To get to that weight I had worked out twice a day and eaten nothing but the limes in my gin and tonics. Even Mary, my trainer and friend, had been worried. I never got so low that I passed out from malnutrition and my friends hovered over my delicate frame and begged me to eat a bagel, please, but I had overshot healthy skinny by about seven pounds. Somewhere in between proving Adam, Susan, and the damn dolphins wrong and those thirty pounds I gained back would have been a perfect weight to maintain.

But when I slowly gained weight back with Jeff it was "happy in love, feeling safe, and not needing to impress anyone else" weight. Jeff always had snacks around, which he would eat over time. But because I was still stuck in my "get them while you can" childhood frame of mind, for me it was no cookies or all the cookies. When we moved in together, Jeff discovered Häagen-Dazs Light mint chip ice cream. He would buy a pint and then I would eat the whole pint, so he started buying two pints—one for me to eat whenever I wanted and one for him to eat whenever he wanted. What would happen instead is that I would finish my pint immediately, and then a few days later, seeing his pint still intact, I would eat that one also. This continued pint after pint yet he was never hostile or judgmental. He never called me Mint Chip Face.

The Häagen-Dazs problem had escalated to the point that one day Jeff came home with four pints. Three for me and one for him. I made my way through my three over the next couple of weeks, keeping an eye on his one pint. He hadn't even touched it! But I had already eaten my three. I couldn't possibly eat his one and only pint. One night when he was off bartending and I was left alone in the apartment, I couldn't take it anymore. Knowing there was a pint of perfectly delicious light mint chip ice cream just sitting there, I opened the freezer and ripped off the plastic lid. A note fell out. A cold little piece of paper that had been placed on top of the ice cream. It was a note from Jeff and all that was on it was a smiley face. I laughed out loud, standing alone in the kitchen. Spork wandered in to see what the commotion was all about and jumped on the counter to get a better look at me laughing so hard I had tears rolling down my face.

Jeff knew me so well, and he accepted me, and he loved me. I was pure happiness in that moment, as I dug my spoon into his pint.

Step 6

Make the Same Mistakes Twice

Adam was small and made me feel fat, even when I wasn't. Jeff was big and made me feel thin, even when I wasn't. Adam was hostile and angry and had a major chip on his shoulder. Jeff was calm and friendly and the only chip on his shoulder was mint. I never wanted to be in another antagonistic relationship where no matter what I said, I was corrected. I didn't want a coach or a competitor. I wanted a boyfriend who would treat me like we were on the same team. I wanted someone I could sit with for five minutes without fighting about what I said, what he said, or whether not helping me get the spilled soy sauce out of the carpet was rude of him, even though he had warned me the cat would knock it off the counter. I wanted someone who would never borrow my car because his was always in the shop and then expect me to walk to a meeting when he drove my car to his.

And I definitely never wanted to date a pot smoker again.

As Jeff drove me home from my twenty-fourth birthday party I was flush with gin, presents, and the excitement that I had chosen to leave with him. We got back to my place, plopped down on the couch, and talked. I am not against casual drug use, or alcohol clearly, since at the moment I was smashed, but my hatred of pot and pot smokers came up. I found them to be self-medicating, annoying, unorganized losers. I told Jeff as much, adding, in true drunken rambling dramatic form, "I want an alpha male! And pot smokers are never alpha males."

It was at this point that twenty-eight-year-old Jeff unapologetically and calmly told me that he had been smoking pot every day since he was sixteen and planned on continuing to do so. He really liked me so it was a shame to end it here, but if I had a problem with his pot consumption, here was where it would end. He started to get up to leave and I straddled him. I looked at his big hazel eyes peeking out of his adorable new glasses and thought, *This probably won't last long anyway. I'm not going to worry about the pot thing right now.* And then I kissed him and he kissed me back. He didn't make it home that night.

As the days rolled into weeks and the weeks rolled into months, I realized I was in yet another relationship with a pot smoker. It also occurred to me that maybe I was so high-strung, only men who were constantly high could be drawn to me. But Jeff was so different from Adam that I convinced myself that their pot habits were incomparable. With Adam, the pot constantly came between us. He was always running late because he had to get stoned. And when he was stoned, he became so affectionate and sweet it just magnified how cold and hostile he was normally. With Jeff I couldn't even tell if he was stoned or not. He was always sweet and even-keeled and no matter how turtle paced, he was always on time. He smoked whenever he wanted, morning until night, but somehow I didn't take it personally. Because the rest of our relationship was so nonconfrontational, the pot didn't become the enemy but instead became a daily part of our lives. Like me talking about Spork's every meow, me eating (or not eating) ice cream, or me freaking out about my career.

All of Jeff's friends were also pot smokers, a slow-moving friendly bunch of Chicago guys who had made it out to Los Angeles for one reason or another. They would lumber over to Jeff's place, since he always seemed to have plenty of weed to go around, plop down, discuss the Bears, kif boxes, and disastrous commercial auditions. Ray, who had thick hair, full, pouty lips, deep blue eyes, and always reminded me of a fat Elvis in the sexiest possible sense, was Jeff's best friend. He was a ridiculously charming, talented actor and from the first night I met him, when he eyed me suspiciously because I wasn't eating any fries, I had the strong sense he knew something I didn't. He and I developed a loving and mildly cantankerous relationship and whenever he looked at me, as he was calmly sitting on the couch, pipe in hand, and I was buzzing around Jeff, I was convinced Ray was thinking, *Come on, Sascha, what are you doing here?*

One night when Jeff and Ray were particularly stoned, and particularly starving, they decided to venture out into the world for pizza. The three of us went to a neighborhood restaurant, sat down in a booth, and ordered immediately. The family sitting in front of us was on their way out, the young boy already racing to the door. In their rush to catch him before he ran into the street and got smushed by a car, they forgot their nearly full box of still hot leftover pizza the waiter had just placed on their table.

Jeff couldn't take his eyes off the box. It was just sitting there, abandoned. Then Jeff said out loud what was abundantly clear.

"I want that pizza."

Ray, because he was just as high as Jeff, and always up for mischief, egged him on.

"Take it. It's just going to get thrown out anyway. Perfectly good pizza. We could eat it, right now. Before our pizza comes."

I was about to be the voice of reason when Jeff reached over and snatched up the box. Then the dad walked back in. Jeff instinctively hid the box under our table as the dad walked over to his old booth looking for the pizza he had forgotten. He kept staring at the table, like the pizza might suddenly appear. Then the waiter came over to him.

"Excuse me, but I forgot our pizza. It was just here a second ago."

"Hmm. Maybe someone took it back to the kitchen."

The waiter went away to see if any of the busboys had picked up the box. The dad waited by his booth. Jeff and Ray were having a fit of hysterical yet silent laughter. The two of them, faces red, big bellies rising and falling to their quiet heaves, were unable to form words or control themselves. Then the mom walked in with the kids.

"What's taking so long?"

"I don't know. They seem to have lost our pizza."

"Lost our pizza? That's outrageous. We were just here."

The waiter came back, asserting no one had touched the pizza. The mom was now furious so the dad had to step up his aggression.

"This is an outrage. That was almost an entire pizza. My son was going to eat that for lunch tomorrow."

"I'm sorry, sir. But I don't know what happened to it."

Amazingly, no one even noticed the two red-eyed, convulsing fat guys in the next booth.

"Well, you are just going to have to make us a new pizza."

It was at this point that my nonstoned brain jumped into action. I felt terrible that the waiter was taking the brunt of our antics so I grabbed the pizza from under our table and, like it was the most normal thing in the world, handed it over to the dad.

"Oh, is this your pizza? I'm so sorry I got confused and thought it was ours and must have accidentally taken it off your table."

The dad took the pizza without asking any questions and once again left the restaurant with his family. The waiter, too busy to really care, ran off to deal with other customers. The silent, stoned howling turned into a ruckus of cackles and Ray, Jeff, and I, forever bonded in pizza-stealing solidarity, laughed until their very own pizza arrived. I had a salad.

Another habit Adam and Jeff shared, which seems to go hand and hand with smoking pot, was playing video games. Adam's game of choice was Resident Evil and whenever I would see his avatar, forever locked in the world of the game and poised to do whatever Adam directed him to do, a wave of loneliness would crash over me. Whenever Adam turned on the game to return to a level he hadn't completed, there was the avatar, waiting patiently, body slightly wobbling, ready to continue on his mission once Adam pressed the button. I decided the lonely feeling wasn't caused by some hole in my soul, but by the scary, slow-moving zombies, the creepy, empty dilapidated towns they infested, and the monotonous tones of the machines guns blasting them into bloody pulps.

When Jeff played video games (none that were zombie-centric), the same feeling washed over me. Eventually I realized it wasn't the game that was making me lonely. I was lonely, and it was the game that made me aware of my feelings. I related not to the player, but to the avatar. The Being frozen in time, whose only purpose is to get more points, pass more levels, and win; unless it is being propelled forward, it's just suspended and useless. So I decided to release the avatar from this prison. And to the amusement of Jeff and Ray, I would take the Grand Theft Auto guy and go for long walks. We would stroll through parks, golf courses, empty buildings, docks, city streets, and quiet suburbs. No points, no levels, no danger, just a nice afternoon out and about, exploring the intricate world of the game. I felt the avatar deserved a break.

When I met Jeff he had this ratty old La-Z-Boy rocker that he had bought for twenty-five bucks at Goodwill. It was like a womb he never wanted to leave. He had a retro silver ashtray right next to his chair, and his pot and pipe, acting as his umbilical cord, lived on the ashtray. He would sit there, gently rocking, watching TV, playing video games, and smoking weed. He was always a very conscientious cigarette smoker and only smoked on the porch. I didn't mind the pot smoke inside the apartment because it actually had a lovely old library smell. So for a while, marijuana and I shared Jeff and lived together in harmony, and I would purge my feelings of loneliness by taking my avatar out for long walks.

Step 7

Think It's Fantastic That Your Significant Other Doesn't Object to You Attending a Party Without Him . . . at the Playboy Mansion

After cheating on Adam and finding it so draining, and in the end, cowardly and completely unjustifiable, I decided to be up-front with Jeff about everything. I told him I had read the Housna letter and had cheated on Adam. I told him I was obsessed with anything purple, and he already knew I had slept with Cody.

When Jeff and I had the taboo but always unavoidable "how many people have you slept with?" conversation, amazingly I told him the truth. Even more amazingly, he was unfazed about any of it. He didn't care that I lost my virginity at thirteen to a gang member. He was amused that I made out with the pool man when I was fourteen.

He was unconcerned that I was a bit of a L.U.G. (Lesbian Until Graduation) in college. Having been a bartender in Chicago for many years, Jeff had seen it all, done it all, and outdone me by dozens. He was not threatened by my past, and because he was so open, had nothing to hide, and had no ex-girlfriends who were seeking political asylum, I wasn't the least bit insecure about his past. We entered into a relationship with complete honesty and no jealousy. I thought this was extraordinarily enlightened of us and would bode well for our relationship's longevity.

We had been dating for three weeks when Jeff walked me to my car after our shift one night. He stood close to me, and he smelled like tobacco and chocolate. He always smelled like tobacco and chocolate. I think it was a natural combination of all the pot, rolled cigarettes, and candy bars, and it was a surprisingly alluring, masculine scent. He looked down at me and somberly said, "Don't take this the wrong way, but—I love you." A shocking thing to hear at all, especially after only three weeks, but I didn't take it the wrong way. I wasn't ready to say it back to him but I didn't run in fear. Instead I nuzzled my face into his yummy-smelling shoulder.

A couple of months later I was laid up with a migraine and Jeff came over after his shift to silently put flowers and a get well card on my doorstep. But I saw him outside and let him in. I'm sure he was exhausted and wanted to go home and sleep in his own bed, but once I asked him to stay, he knew he was stuck. We curled up in bed and as my head pounded and my right eye felt like it was going to explode all over the pillow, I thought, *Here is a man who brings me flowers when I have a migraine, instead of stealing my pills! Here is a man who is thoughtful and kind and weighs a good seventy pounds more than me! Here is a man that I love.* I told him so.

It was around this time that we both established we were going to be committed—to each other, not into an insane asylum. Then, four months into dating, I was invited to go to the Playboy Mansion for Hef's lingerie-themed seventieth birthday party. My friend Mimi, one of the waitresses at the Improv I had been known to flirt with, was invited by a guy she knew, and that guy was bringing another guy who needed a date. Mimi asked if I wanted to be that date.

Usually when you're dating someone, under no circumstances could you go to the Playboy Mansion on a double date, wearing lingerie, when neither of the other guys was your boyfriend. But since going to the mansion was a dream of mine, I couldn't pass it up. I had a long and intense love of *Playboy*. My childhood fascination with hookers led to curiosity about the sex trade in general—burlesque dancers, strippers, soft-core porn on Showtime, Dr. Ruth advice, and anything untoward. Susan always encouraged my interests, no matter what they were, and would wake me up in the middle of the night if there was a documentary on Gypsy Rose Lee, Bettie Page, or the Dance of the Seven Veils. She taught me about sex in the context of history, social mores, and trends and never made me feel ashamed that I was intrigued by the subject. She felt prudes were the ones who should be ashamed.

I was certainly aware of *Playboy* growing up, but it wasn't until I was bedridden for six weeks and recovering from mild post-traumatic stress syndrome that I fell in love with *Playboy*.

December 3, 1996. I was twenty years old (post meeting Adam but pre dating him), and I had planned to take a train to Rhode Island that evening. Susan starting calling me that morning with uncharacteristic concern, telling me to "be careful" and "have a safe trip." Susan, the same mother who shipped me off to sleep-away camp when I was only five, wasn't fazed when she found beer under my bed in junior high, let me travel around England unchaperoned when I was fourteen (and I got a shoddy tattoo of a heart on my right hip), and told me to "never shoot up heroin; only snort it if you must." Susan, who could be accused of neglect far more than overprotectiveness, was now concerned about me taking a forty-five–minute train trip from Boston to Providence. I asked her why and she couldn't say exactly.

"Just a feeling."

Susan almost never had feelings.

It wasn't like me to plan last-minute trips, especially on a school night. But it was my best friend Jennifer's twenty-first birthday and her grandmother died that day. I first met Jennifer when I was five years old, in kindergarten. I hated her. She was petite and proper and had a better vocabulary than me. She still does. Which is maybe why she got into Brown and I didn't get into Yale, which in turn is why I ended up at Boston College. But that's not the point and I'm certainly not bitter about it.

In first grade we both wanted the same chair in the library.

"That's my chair."

"I don't see your name written on it."

We nudged each other and during the scuffle my beaded necklace broke. Jennifer cried because she felt responsible and didn't want to get into trouble. I cried because it wasn't really my beaded necklace at all. It was Berns's. That morning I had crept into her supercool room, riffled through her awesome things, and borrowed it without permission. Tiny little translucent beads poured over the library floor and Jennifer and I both scrambled to pick them up through our guilty tears. That moment brought us together and was the start of a lifelong friendship.

When I left public elementary school for private in fourth grade, Jennifer and I remained inseparable. She was my one true friend during the big fat ugly sausage days. I would stay at her house Friday nights, and she would stay at mine Saturday nights. We would wash our hair with Finesse shampoo, play hours and hours of jacks, and cackle about everything from bad words to cute boys to the plantar wart on my big toe that I named Mortimer.

So Jennifer needed me on December third because she was a mess. She was already drunk trying to celebrate her most important birthday to date, and she was sobbing because her grandmother had died. She loved her grandmother. Jennifer loved lots of people and wasn't afraid to say it. She said "I love you" to her mom and dad and brother constantly: getting off the phone, getting out of the car, every morning before school. She even said "I love you" to extended family members. I tried to convince myself it was nothing but sentimental drivel, but I knew it was more. It was genuine. Jennifer even said "I love you" to me. It took years and years to get used to it but eventually I started saying it back, though never in front of Susan.

So after getting off the phone with Susan for the eighth time that night I headed to the Amtrak station in Boston and took a train to Providence. I planned on spending a few hours with Jennifer and then taking the last train of the night back. I couldn't be late because if I missed that train, I wouldn't get back to Boston until the next morning, and I would miss my History of Theater class and I never missed class. I was a chronic list-making, diary-keeping, compulsively neat, straight-A student.

After eating Mexican food and bar hopping with Jennifer and her gaggle of roommates, I arrived at the Providence train station. As I rushed down the stairs to my platform, I saw my train pulling out. *How is this possible? Am I late? Is it leaving early? I have to get on that train! If I miss class my whole world will fall apart. It will be anxiety-fueled anarchy!* I noticed one of the doors was flapping open and closed as the train rumbled ahead.

"Don't jump!"

The lone man's warning was too late. I had already jumped.

I actually thought, *How hard can it be? People do it in movies all the time.* What I didn't factor in was that I was not a professional stuntwoman, that the enormous size of the train made it appear to be moving slower than it actually was, and, oh, yeah, that I was wearing five-inch platform boots. I was also carrying an oversize brown and white faux fur cow print bag that Berns had made for me. Yes, it was the midnineties and faux fur was in.

The right side of my body cleared the opening in the door, no problem. It was the left side that was the issue. My left leg got stuck in the gap. The gap we are all supposed to mind.

All I could think was, *This isn't happening to me.*

As my left leg got sucked deeper and deeper into the gap, I lost my barely established balance completely. My right hand couldn't hold on to the door frame anymore and my entire body swung around out of the train. I was screaming. I was now crammed in the small space between the concrete platform and the enormous speeding metal locomotive.

I can't believe this is happening to me.

I had heard stories about people getting stuck in gaps. It occurs every couple of years in New York City. A person gets trapped and spun around and around until all their insides are mush, while they are still conscious. Their loved ones are notified and rush to the tracks to say one last good-bye. Then, because nothing can be done, once the train leaves the station and all the pressure is removed, the organs in the lower half of their body fall out and the person dies. I always wondered what kind of moron gets caught in the gap. You would have to be really clumsy or really stupid to fall into such an enormously avoidable predicament.

My body was smashed and spinning in the gap for a few seconds, which seemed interminable, and then somehow squeezed through, falling onto the train tracks below. There was grinding, screeching metal everywhere and the noise was deafening.

I am going to die.

Once I accepted I was going to die it was actually the most relaxing moment of my life. All my anxiety dissolved. Making sure my purple pens were placed perpendicularly on my desk seemed pointless. Fretting all day that I might have left a tiny glob of toothpaste on the sink was a waste of energy. Perfect grades didn't matter. Avoiding uttering clichés at dinner parties didn't matter. Succeeding didn't matter. Losing five pounds didn't matter. There was nothing more to worry about.

In high school I waitressed at a cute diner and every so often I would put too many drinks on one tray, trying to overachieve. And as I slowly walked that tray to an eight-top, I was filled with dread that the drinks would topple onto the customers. Once the first drink starts to tip, it's all over. You can try to recover and save some of the glasses, but, like dominoes, once the balance of the tray is thrown off, the chain of events can't be stopped so you just have to let it go. You apologize to the customers, give them a free dessert, get some napkins, and sweep away the broken glass, and then it's over. Looming death was like that tray of drinks. Once I accepted it was going to happen, that the glasses were going to fall, the dread was gone, and I let it all go. I had reached nirvana.

The second I landed on the tracks, there was a break in the cars, but a new set of wheels was only a breath away from severing me in half. But in that very breath, some other instinct kicked in. The instinct that did care about the toothpaste glob and being skinny and that wasn't okay with just dropping the tray and accepting death. Without realizing it, I willed myself to move and flopped over the side of the tracks toward the platform just before the wheels could slice me to pieces. The tracks were built on a mound, a few feet lower than the platform. This allows the height of the train to match the height of the platform, so people can easily step onto the train when it isn't moving. When I tossed my body off the tracks, I rolled down the mound and landed on my back, six feet under the platform. The train, a few feet in front of me and six feet above me, rumbled on.

The first thing I noticed were the giant rats scurrying over my body. Dirty, germ-infested, rabid rats, but I didn't care. The second thing I noticed was that my head was incredibly comfortable. I slowly moved my neck to the side and realized my giant faux fur bag had swung up during my fall and landed first, right behind my head, acting as a plush cow-printed pillow. That bag kept me conscious.

That bag saved me from any head trauma. That bag saved my life. Berns saved my life! The third thing I noticed was that I couldn't move my legs.

My positive attitude was gone.

Oh my God, I'm paralyzed. I'm stuck in a crevice six feet under a train track and I can't move my legs! And there are rats all over me! I tried to calm myself down and think. . . . *If I can move my toes in my boots, then I'm not paralyzed.* I took a deep breath and wiggled my toes. They were moving and I could feel them moving! I was not paralyzed. I was frantically elated.

"Are you alive?!"

It was the man who had told me not to jump. He was screaming down to me from the platform. I couldn't see him, but I could hear him now that the train, and its deafening rumble, had stopped.

"Yes, I'm alive! I'm alive!"

"Do you have your legs?"

"Yes!"

"I can't believe you have your legs!"

"I can't believe I'm alive!"

And I couldn't. I was now euphoric. I was scared and on some distant level I knew I was in pain, but I was the strongest, fastest, smartest moron in the whole world. I had survived getting dragged under a train.

But why? Why did I have my legs? Why was I alive? I never believed in God and thought it would be hypocritical to start now. Was it luck? Fate? Did I have some purpose in life I hadn't yet fulfilled? My mind raced. Other than some cursory volunteer work in my junior year of high school, done solely to beef up my college applications, I'd never had any real interest in helping anyone. I was selfish, spoiled, and unsympathetic to the world's suffering. But this near-death experience was going to change me. I would be a better person, never take anything for granted again. I would go to Ethiopia and help the children.

The train, which had stopped for a few minutes, now rumbled away, leaving the tracks open. The man who had seen me jump worked for Amtrak and he had found a way down under the platform and was now standing over me. He covered me with a blanket and told me an ambulance was on the way. I told him I was going to Ethiopia to help the children.

I think I must have been in shock, and the shock was wearing off. Or maybe the shock was just starting, because I began to shiver uncontrollably. It was at this point that I realized I was going to miss class.

The ambulance arrived and within minutes several hot EMT guys were hunched over me, checking my vital signs and asking questions.

"What's your name? How old are you? Do you have any allergies or preexisting medical conditions? Have you been drinking?"

The honest answer to that last question was no. Jennifer was plastered and I thought I should be sober to better take care of her, and it was a school night, so I hadn't had even one drink. Had I been drinking, at least

I would have an excuse as to why I thought it wise to jump onto a moving train. Embarrassingly, I was totally sober.

The hot guys put a brace around my neck and gingerly slid a small narrow board under my back. They explained they had to get me out of there with as little movement as possible since I might have a spinal cord injury. After much thought the only solution was to lift me vertically back up through the very space through which I had fallen. Now that there was no train, it was a much larger area. Two of the EMTs went back up onto the platform and two stayed with me in the ditch. They then lifted me, two men pushing me up through the gap while the two on the platform pulled me to safety—four big, strong men rescuing me from my impulsive decision. It was incredibly romantic and exciting.

At that moment instead of panicking about the state of my spinal cord or the fact that my left leg was drenched in blood or worrying about the children in Ethiopia, I fretted about my weight. I actually sucked in my stomach. Was I too heavy? Did they think I was fat? I shouldn't have eaten that burrito.

In the emergency room, after hours of tests and catheters and scans and needles, it was established that I was stable. I had a crushed pelvis, severe bruising, and minor abrasions. But I was going to live, and I was insanely lucky. When I called Susan and John to tell them what had happened, Susan answered, wide awake. She was just sitting there in the middle of the night waiting for the call. She had a feeling, and she was right.

I not only missed my History of Theater class, but I missed a lot of classes and all of my finals. Once I was released from the hospital, I flew home and I didn't move for six weeks, other than using a wheelchair to get from the bed to the bathroom. I just lay there. My mind raced. The painkillers kept me in a fog but they also made me nauseous, so I stopped taking them. I had constant nightmares about getting eaten by giant metal whales. Reading took too much concentration. I couldn't focus on the schoolwork I would have to eventually make up and watching TV was too upsetting. Everywhere I looked there were car chases, airplane crashes, bustling, grinding city noises.

While desperately searching for something to turn my mind off, I discovered one TV channel that I could watch. One channel that soothed my post-traumatic–stressed soul: the Playboy Channel.

Watching pretty girls with long, luxuriously tacky acrylic nails, white-blond hair, and giant fake boobs making out with each other was just the thing I needed. It was mindless, calming, and totally mesmerizing. There was no violence on the Playboy Channel. Nothing moved too quickly, and there were no jarring noises, only the moans of fake orgasms. Watching it hour after hour kept my mind away from the meaning of life, the pain in my bones, and the feeling that I was both invincible and yet totally fragile at the same time.

Susan would watch the Playboy Channel with me. We would curl up on my makeshift convalescence bed in the library and discuss the inane dialogue, which shade of pink lipstick was best, and the pros and cons of doing it in a hot tub. John was horrified that I was watching Playboy all day, but he was more horrified that Susan was watching it with me. He threatened to cancel the channel, which he denied ever specifically ordering in the first place, but I convinced him it was the only thing that was going to keep me sane over the next six bedridden weeks. So it stayed.

By the time I recovered and went back to college, I was an avid fan. Adam's mother got me a subscription to the magazine as a present. When I moved off campus my senior year and lived in a house with three guys, I was the one to order and pay for the Playboy Channel.

So when the opportunity presented itself to go to the mansion for Hef's seventieth birthday party, I couldn't say no. I told Mimi to tell her friend's friend that I had a boyfriend. I told Jeff to please stay at my place that night so when I got home from the party, I could put all that glittered-bunny, heated-grotto, anything-goes sexual energy onto him.

Our plan went off without a hitch. I went to the party and had an amazing time seeing the painted ladies, the famous game room, the bird sanctuary, the forgotten celebrities, the Playmates, and of course Hef himself. At three a.m., seeing that things were starting to get racy, I left Mimi and the boys and took a cab home. I walked in and there was Jeff, sitting on my couch, watching TV and smoking pot. I told him all about the party and then we fooled around.

One day, a year into our relationship, I was feeling

particularly frisky and kept running into gorgeous guys everywhere—the car wash, the Coffee Bean, the gym. I wanted to keep our total honesty with each other going, so at dinner that night I said to Jeff, "I want to sleep with everyone today!" He responded, "That's okay. When you blow me I don't think about you anymore."

That night we had sex knowing full well we were thinking of others. And there was comfort in that. We didn't need to lie to each other. We didn't need to pretend we didn't find other people attractive or that the sex was as hot as it used to be. We were confident enough in our relationship to be honest about sex. And in that honesty there was total commitment to each other. Or so we thought.

Step 8

Believe Your Differences Make Things More Interesting

From day one Jeff and I clearly saw each other's differences, but we reveled in our opposites. Just like the Paula Abdul song "Opposites Attract," where she sings, "Who'da thought we could be lovers?" Except instead of "She makes the bed, and he steals the covers," I liked to go out, Jeff didn't. He liked to smoke pot, I didn't. He was a meat-and-potatoes-eating, plaid-shirt-wearing, baseball-obsessed Chicago guy. I was a turkey-burger-and-salad-eating, pointy-boots-wearing, reality-show-obsessed Miami Beach girl. We pushed those inherent differences aside, thinking they were just superficial, and we were determined to make the relationship work. Because deep down in our cores, we believed we were the same.

We both understood that even when you get a complimentary entrée for whatever reason at a restaurant, you still tip the waiter twenty percent on what the meal would have cost. We were extremely cynical when it came to organized religion, self-help books, and Dr. Phil advice. We loved to hate Successories posters, guided tours of anything, and people who say "Have a blessed day" on their answering machines. We had the same dark, nothing-is-sacred sense of humor. We both disliked children and planned never to have them. And those last two things led us to jokingly pick out a nice abortion clinic, in case I ever did get pregnant. We were driving to see our happily married lawyer friends in Altadena and when we happened to pass by a clinic in Pasadena, we both remarked how quiet and peaceful it seemed. When we got to our friends' house we gleefully said, "We found the perfect abortion place!" They were appalled, which made Jeff and me feel like true soul mates.

When we started dating I asked Jeff to teach me how to roll cigarettes. Not because I smoked (it was the one and only thing Susan ever asked me not to do, since her first husband had died of lung cancer), but because Jeff looked so damn cool doing it. He walked me through pinching a bit of tobacco out of the bag, placing it gingerly on the paper, rolling it up between my thumb and my fingers with one quick motion, licking the sticky part, and sealing it up. I became really good at it and was appointed his official roller when he was driving. He was perfectly capable of driving and rolling at the same time, but he liked when I did it for him. And I liked it too. Although I knew with each cigarette he was one step closer to destroying his lungs, I was proud to be a part of his daily routine. It was a way for me to feel a little closer to him. Like we were in it together, even though we were so different.

A major disparity in our personalities wasn't just that Jeff smoked pot and I didn't, but that we actually had very different drugs of choice. His was obviously marijuana. Mine was cocaine. And although I hadn't done coke since I was thirteen years old, it didn't change the fact that I inherently gravitated toward uppers, and Jeff gravitated toward downers. I wanted to feel even faster, stronger, smarter, chattier, twitchier, and more anxious than my natural, drug-free state. He wanted to feel even slower, weaker, calmer, stiller, and dumber than his usual self. Pot energy versus coke energy magnified how different we were, but joining the two worked to cool me off and to ramp him up. I wasn't actually doing coke at that time, but still, I became his upper and he became my downer.

In a nutshell, our biggest difference was that I tried too hard and he didn't try at all. At my twenty-fourth birthday party I told Jeff I wanted to be and would be the girl in the box at the Standard Hotel. A few weeks later, I found out who was in charge of hiring those girls and I made an appointment. I stood in front of Trevor, an ultra hipster gay guy wearing white loafers and a studded belt. He gave me a once-over, asked me to turn around in a circle, and then told me to look bored. After my thirty-second audition he said, "Okay, you can start Monday night." The pay was ten dollars an hour for an eight-hour shift. All I had to do was lie in a giant glass tank in the middle of a hotel lobby. Awesome!

Jeff was astounded that I did what I said I wanted to do. It's rare anywhere, and especially in L.A., to meet someone who actually follows through, and he said he was inspired by my fearless conquering of my goals: moving to L.A. a week after college graduation to pursue a writing career, hammering through spec scripts to get an agent, quitting my cushy TV assistant job after a year because I was losing sight of my dreams, becoming the girl in the tank.

That Monday I lay in the big glass box wearing the uniform of a tight white tank top and white boy shorts. I was instructed, above all else, to act totally bored. People who go to the Standard Hotel are already cool, so in order for me to be even cooler, and worthy of the tank, I had to seem utterly over it all. I painted my nails, talked on my cell, slept, did anything mundane I could think of to pass the time. All the while making no eye contact with the people who were outside the tank, staring at me. I was instructed not only to look over them but to look through them.

I appeared completely disinterested but inside that tank and inside my soul I was thrilled to be deemed skinny and beautiful enough to be gazed upon. I was exhilarated to be thought attractive enough to become an object. And I was teeming with excitement and anything but bored. I wondered if the other tank girls were so used to being beautiful and objectified that they were in fact not acting bored but actually were bored.

Jeff came to look at me in the tank. He brought a paper, sat in the lobby, did the crossword puzzle, and glanced up at me every so often. I looked out at him and realized I was trying to look bored in order to be cooler than all the people trying to look cool, and he wasn't trying to look anything. He was just sitting there in his ugly plaid shirt, crumpled trench coat, and sneakers (and not the trendy kind). But because he wasn't trying, he was inherently so much cooler than everyone else, including me. Even though I was in the tank and he was in the lobby he was so much more secure than me. So much more centered. I was inspired to stop trying so hard and try to just be me.

For a long time that balance of me pushing him to accomplish what he wanted and him pulling me back from my frantic precipice worked very well for us both. I motivated him to get new head shots, take acting classes, audition for plays. And he almost convinced me it was okay to breathe, sit, and try to enjoy the present instead of always freaking out about the unknown future. I motivated him to start exercising. He motivated me to stop wearing see-through clothes. Our opposite personalities were making us both a little better.

In the beginning, we each branched out and tried doing things the other enjoyed. I watched a few Bears games, went to a Cubs game, and ate at his favorite restaurant, Fuddruckers. He went to a few dance clubs, wore his "good jeans," and ate at my favorite restaurant, Urth Caffé. But as time passed, we became comfortable enough with the relationship to stop doing things just to please the other person and stuck with the things we liked, individually. So, although we still had happy times curled up in bed, we didn't spend any time together out in the world.

In our denial, we decided this was the perfect relationship. We never had to do anything we didn't want to do. I would never be one of those girls who would drag him to see a romantic comedy. He would never be one of those guys who had to sit uncomfortably in the lone chair in a boutique watching his girlfriend try on little black dresses that all look the same. We were proud that we never had to go anywhere together. I would attend work parties, go out for drinks, go to birthdays, gallery openings, and brunches, always solo. At first all my friends would ask, "Where's Jeff?" After a while they stopped asking. No one expected him to be by my side, including me. I always invited him, and it would have been nice for him to join me, but I was fine without him.

I got the impression some of the boyfriends of my friends were a little envious of Jeff and I took that as a compliment. Jeff was allowed to miss the group dinners where there is always someone who doesn't pay enough when the check comes, avoid the small talk about gym memberships, hide from the gossip about who was having a nervous breakdown, and stay away from all the L.A. posturing and name-dropping. Everyone would always say, "Tell Jeff I say hi. I really like that guy." And everyone did really like him. The rare times he was out, he was always charming and gracious and funny. He spent so little time with my friends that they only saw him on his very best behavior. And after a while, he not only didn't want to spend a lot of time with my friends, but he didn't want to spend a lot of time with me.

Major issues arose with him wanting "alone time" and me wanting "us time." He's the ultimate introvert and his battery recharges when he's alone. I'm the ultimate extrovert and my battery depletes unless I'm with others. And according to him, because he expended so much energy bartending, being übercharming and social, he was exhausted on his nights off. And because I was always seeing friends and being social without him, I expected his nights away from the bar to be with me. When I would come home from my various solo social activities, I would want to curl up on Jeff's lap, in his giant chair, and tell him about my adventures while he slowly rocked back and forth and watched TV. It was a comforting stillness sitting there on him, far away from the bustling world.

Over the months and years rules and regulations were created. After seven months of dating, Jeff declared he needed more alone time. So he got three "nights off" a week. Not from the bar, but from me. It didn't occur to me until it was too late that this phrasing made spending time with me sound like work. Unpleasant work at that. Not good for relationship morale.

My diary entries started to address my concern.

Why do I feel bad when Jeff doesn't want to spend time with me? Why am I so insecure that I think every minute apart means less love? We went

81

from three nights on and one night off to three nights off and one night on. Why do I want to spend time with someone who doesn't want to spend time with me? It's pathetic. At least Spork is here.

One week, after (shockingly) spending a few days in a row together, Jeff had reached his "us time" limit and told me he felt like a "sponge that couldn't absorb any more dirty water." If he was the sponge and I was the water, why did I have to be dirty? He thought of spending time with me like slowly drinking up dank dishwater! The second it came out of his mouth he felt terrible and said, "See, that's what happens when my battery is out: I have no filter." He apologized and squished me and then I went home to give him some alone time to recharge. But the thing about filters is, whether you choose to say what you are thinking or not, you are still thinking it, and once it has come out, you can't take it back.

And although I convinced myself and others I was independent and it didn't bother me that Jeff never wanted to go anywhere, it eventually created a divide. The more time I spent without him, the more I realized I didn't need him, or even want him. Once that happens it's hard to ever go back. I continued to invite him out, but an imperceptible shift was happening. When he would say, "No, thanks, but I'll be here when you get back," instead of being disappointed, I was relieved.

Step 9

Resent Each Other

A year and a half into our relationship, at the height of the fights about alone time and dirty-dishwater-saturated sponges, I was offered a job traveling around the country interviewing stupid people for a game show called *Street Smarts*. For the next six months I would be out of town for three weeks, then have a week in L.A. before heading back out on the road. I took the job because it sounded like a fun adventure, it would allow me time to write on nontravel weeks, and it paid well. I wasn't worried about leaving Jeff for weeks at a time because he wanted to be alone anyway, but I was worried about Spork.

I had had Spork for three years. After Adam had moved in with me and passed his California medical exam, he started working at a hospital, and late one night someone dropped a box of tiny kittens off there. Most were adopted immediately. But Spork, funny looking, gangly

83

legged, and all black, was left in the little box. When I met him he crawled up my arm and nestled on my collarbone. I knew he was mine. Adam put some cream on his runny eye, and I took him home. I sat in front of the tiny bundle of black fur and watched as he awkwardly fell all over himself playing with the carpet. After a few names were uttered—Renfield, Faust, Pork—I stumbled upon Spork and it stuck.

Maybe Spork and I fell for each other because we are both neurotic, high-strung, paranoid beings. Or maybe living with me turned him into that kind of cat. Spork is afraid of new people, garbage truck noises, and ceiling fans. He sometimes frantically runs from room to room for no apparent reason. At night he patrols the apartment, opening up all the cabinets and doors. His favorite spot to lounge is wedged between my laptop and the lip of my desk. When he sleeps, splayed out to the right of my pillow every night, he looks more like a beached seal than a cat. He meows like a film noir sidekick and plays fetch with little toy mice, which I often find nestled in the sheets. Spork is not the cat who will lazily come out and socialize with strangers. He is the cat who will make a mad dash under the bed when anyone comes to the door. But after months of someone being around day in and day out, he might warm up. This behavior makes his love for me all the more special, and it makes leaving him very traumatic for us both. I worry that he will die of a broken heart, and he worries that I might never come back.

By the time of the *Street Smarts* job, Spork and Jeff had

a nice rapport. I knew Jeff wouldn't mind coming over to feed him from time to time, but that wasn't enough for me to feel guilt-free about leaving. I came up with a plan so Spork wouldn't be alone for weeks on end. I bought a PlayStation 2 and set it up at my apartment. Then I bought *Final Fantasy XI*. I told Jeff that after my six-month travel stint, the console and game were his to take home. In the meantime, he would have to play at my place. Ray, whom Spork had also come to accept, was welcome to park himself on my couch for half a year and play as well. I knew this arrangement would keep Jeff occupied and stationary for months, and Spork would have hours and hours of company.

It was on *Street Smarts* that I met Michelle, a beautiful girl my age with delicate features, luminous caramel skin, and a laugh like a drunken sailor. Our first night on the road we found ourselves huddled together in the corner of a Lake Havasu Holiday Inn discotheque. We watched the methed-out locals and trashed Fourth of July partiers dance to an endless remix of Kid Rock screaming "I'll fuck you blind, bitch, I'll fuck you blind, bitch, I'll fuck you 'til you just can't see no more."

Over the next six months Michelle and I traveled around the United States and bonded. We both had tell-it-like-it-is mothers and performer boyfriends. She was dating a comic from Pittsburgh. Our significant others had their similarities. We discussed our own hopes and dreams and fears, we played tic-tac-toe against a chicken in Vegas (the chicken won), and we went to the Mall of

America and gawked at all the women wearing opaque tan stockings with open-toed shoes. We went to a black rodeo in Orange County, a stock car race in Henderson, and a hippie fair in Seattle. We went to Chicago and stood on Wrigley Field right before a Cubs game. I called Jeff at that moment to tell him I was two feet away from Sammy Sosa. He knew the momentousness was lost on me but was happy I tried to share it with him anyway. I also called Jeff every night, from countless hotels, to say "Sweet dreams."

The day after my final *Street Smarts* trip Jeff, Spork, and I were on the balcony, having our morning coffee, when Jeff said, "I've been thinking, we should move in together." All it took was for me to give him a lot of alone time for him to realize he no longer wanted any. So after two years of dating we both decided it was time to move in together. But that left one big decision for us to agree on—where.

At that time I was living in a nice, clean third-story one bedroom with underground parking in Miracle Mile. I was blocks away from all my closest friends and in five minutes could be chatting with them over coffee, hiking up Runyon Canyon, or getting a pedicure. That neighborhood is just south of Hollywood, very central and surrounded by fun bars and restaurants and museums. Jeff lived in a grimy room with a hot plate, barely a bathroom, and no parking, twenty feet from the ocean in Venice Beach. That part of Los Angeles is on the edge of the Earth, far from everything and surrounded by the beach, the grime, and the homeless hippies. Although Venice and Miracle Mile are only ten miles apart, they seem like worlds apart. And of course Jeff, a pot-smoking, land-locked Chicago guy, loved being by the ocean: the cool, smog-free breeze, the sunsets, and the unassuming hippies (who are in actuality really annoying and self-important). But since I grew up on the beach, I had no appreciation for it. I never liked the scratchy sand, the salty ocean water, or the peeling tourists, and I stayed out of the sun at all costs because of skin cancer concerns and my desire to be vampire pale. I would much rather be around the clearly fake Hollywood types than the pseudo-spiritual fake Venice types.

But I was looking forward to living with Jeff, putting an end to the constant overnight bags, the nights without Spork, and the alone time battles, so I gave up my beloved Miracle Mile and headed west.

We rented a cute, two-bedroom bungalow on the Venice canals. We had one parking spot, which was deemed mine, and a small patio that was Jeff's smoking area and Spork's sunning area. The smaller of the bedrooms was my office, and the living room housed Jeff's chair, ashtray, and the TV. The move-in was seamless.

Now that we lived together, and Jeff technically didn't get any nights off, new rules were instated. I was not allowed to talk to him too much when he got home from the bar. He wanted to sit in his chair, smoke pot, and peacefully watch TV. In the mornings, I was not allowed to talk to him until he had had at least one cigarette and two cups of coffee. Only after that "the questions" could start. Yes, I was a little frantic, a little demanding and high-strung. And maybe I tried too hard. But not being able to talk until the appointed time made me even more anxious. So when he finished the last drop of that second cup, I would bounce over to him and begin.

"How did you sleep? I had the weirdest dream. Spork was on a boat with us and there was a fireman shoving salt in my mouth. What are you doing today? Did you call the plumber yet? I'm meeting Jennifer for lunch. Do you want me to bring you something? What time does the game start? I know you hate these things, but will you please go with me to Jason's birthday party for just twenty minutes?"

Jeff would take a big belly sigh and start talking in his gravely deep morning voice. I loved that voice.

For most of our relationship I was like Chester, the small, yippy, energetic cartoon terrier, and Jeff was like Spike, the big, lumbering, bowler-hat-wearing cartoon bulldog. When we realized this was our dynamic I would literally jump up and down next to Jeff, saying, "What are we gonna do now, Spike? What are we gonna do now?" This was most fun when we were in the grocery store or in the mall or running errands of any kind. Jeff always played his part of the slowly grumbling Spike counting the minutes and objectives before he could get back in his chair. I played my part of being rambunctious and excited and time efficient enough for the both of us.

When Ray was around, it was like having two Spikes, so my Chester just doubled in energy.

Not shockingly, Jeff's laid-back attitude lent itself to being messy and unorganized. He left clothes everywhere, stacks of books and heads shots on every surface, his change and rolling paper pell-mell all over counters. I gave him certain areas where he could house all of his runaway items. So when doing my hourly walk-through of the apartment, I would take his random sock, lighter, Subway receipt, stained baseball cap, five-dollar bill, and plastic thingy that fell off his car door, and place them all inside one of his appointed drawers. He never minded me putting his things away and binding them together like a corset on a plump maiden. And I didn't resent him being messy, because it was fun for me to constantly organize and clean and hide away anything not supposed to be out.

One area that was left solely to his discretion was his car. It was his car, after all. I'm not sure if it was such a disaster because I kept the apartment so neat, or if it would have been a disaster regardless, but his Honda looked like a family of carnival workers might have been living in there for years. My car, on the other hand, looked as though it had never even been test-driven. If a penny fell out of my bag and behind the seat I would pull over and find it and put it back in my change purse. If a water bottle found its way into the cup holder, I would take it out immediately upon arriving at my destination. I had my car washed every week and hated clutter so much, I wouldn't even keep my Thomas Guide, a necessary map if you live in a city as giant as Los Angeles, in the backseat. I kept it hidden in the trunk, rendering it useless when I got lost.

So based on the state of our cars alone it was clear what we were all about. I was about control, order, and neatness. Jeff was about soda cans, beach towels, candy wrappers, tobacco remnants, and rolling paper.

It would stand to reason that Jeff and I were so completely opposite that our taste in décor would also be conflicting, but he and I devised a fair and brilliant system when we moved in together. Most of our items came from my end, including beautiful antique furniture from my grandparents on Susan's side. Marble-top dressers, chaise lounges, and nineteenth-century French Napoleon chairs might not have been the first thing Jeff would buy for himself, but he didn't complain about them. He arrived with only his La-Z-Boy chair, his silver ashtray, and a bookshelf. The trouble was the artwork.

There were a few things of mine he liked, like the picture of a woman in a garter belt bending down in a pumpkin patch, and a few things of his I liked, like the whimsical café on a cobbled street painting. For the rest, Jeff and I decided that we could each pick one thing from the other's pile that would not be hung up. He picked my favorite painting. A Matisse-looking five-by-four-foot canvas of a woman flopped over a lion-shaped fountain with an inexplicable red lobster floating in the upper right corner. A boy had painted it for Berns when they were in college. I always coveted it, as I did most of her things, and she gave it to me a few years after receiving it.

Jeff hated that painting, which I found surprising, because I thought it was endlessly interesting to gaze upon. What didn't surprise Jeff was the item of his I picked to not be hung up, a giant framed poster of a hot dog in a bun being airlifted down onto Navy Pier. The poster was something you might see in an orange, red, and yellow-painted Chicago diner. Floating off the pier by the hot dog were barges filled with tomatoes, onions, and relish. A giant pickle was also floating toward the pier.

So the hot dog and lobster artwork were put in a closet, and all seemed good. I enjoyed watching the ducks on the canals, especially in the spring when they were followed by dozens of ducklings that looked like tiny floating fuzz droplets. I relaxed during my evening jogs on the beach, when the sun had just set and the usually crowded boardwalk had thinned out, and I even began to appreciate the feel of the clean beach air.

But after a few months I felt isolated from my friends who were mere miles away. Frustrated that I was so far from everything I knew and loved, I felt lonelier now that I was living with Jeff.

I couldn't put my finger on why I felt so alone, so instead I just blamed it all on Venice, and I loved complaining about it. Now I was unhappy living in Venice, but happy to have something to complain about. Jeff was happy living in Venice, and unhappy I had something to complain about. Jeff and I almost never actually fought.

It was what went unsaid that seemed to be our problem, and what went unsaid was my building resentment at having rules about when I could and couldn't talk to him and at living where he wanted to live and still feeling alone and his building resentment at my wanting to punish him for it.

Step 10

Adhere to an Arbitrary Timetable

In the back of my mind, no matter how independent, non-traditional, and nondomestic I pretended to be, I always had a timetable. Date for two years, then move in together. If that goes well, get engaged at three years, and then get married. I wasn't the girl who pictured her wedding dress or ever considered changing her last name, but I had this notion that twenty-seven was the perfect age to get married. When I was eleven I decided that at that point I would be old enough to know what I wanted, make good decisions, and understand the responsibility of being in love. I was wrong.

While I was dating Jeff I would have vehemently denied all this timetable stuff because I despised girls who wanted to get married just for the sake of marriage. But, as with all the other established goals in my life, I was purposefully pursuing this one as well.

Jennifer came by one day to pick me up for a girls'

outing of lunch and shopping. She walked into the living room beaming and casually tossed her left hand in the air. I saw a gleaming diamond engagement ring. I started squealing, loudly.

"Oh, my God! When? How?"

"Last night. We were having dinner at this hotel and Greg led me up to the rooftop and we were looking at the amazing view and all of a sudden he is on one knee!"

"Ahhhhhhh!"

Jeff, still asleep because he had had a long bartending shift the night before, shuffled out of the bedroom and in a grumpy yet concerned tone asked, "What's going on here? What's wrong?"

"Jennifer got engaged!"

"Oh. That's great. I'm going back to bed."

Jeff disappeared back into the bedroom, shutting the door a little too forcefully.

That night I wrote in my diary.

I'm despondent. Maybe it's just PMS but I want someone to love me enough to propose to me and to marry me. But then I wonder, why do I want to get married? It would be exciting for a little while, but then life takes over. I need to write. I need to go to the gym. I need to sell a script. I want Jeff to book something soon. I want lots of money and a big diamond ring and for Jeff to be successful and to be skinny. Me to be skinny, not Jeff. Is that too much to ask?

The night before our three-year anniversary, one week before my twenty-seventh birthday, I stayed up fantasizing about how Jeff might propose, the ring he would painstakingly pick out for me, and how we would shop for a condo together. Jeff hadn't done anything remotely romantic since the sour apple Blow Pop days, so I'm not sure why I was expecting his entire personality to change all of a sudden. But since I had so long ago decided three years was the time to get engaged, it didn't occur to me that Jeff wasn't in on my plans. It didn't occur to me that he hadn't been slowly saving up for a ring and it didn't occur to me that he hadn't called Berns months before to get her input on the four Cs: color, cut, clarity, and carat.

By the end of the next day it was apparent that not only was Jeff not planning on proposing, he had actually forgotten it was our anniversary. I kept thinking he was just pretending to have forgotten to make the reveal so much more unexpected. But nothing happened. No ring, no champagne, no getting down on one knee. None of the horrible clichés I was embarrassed to admit I so desperately wanted.

I yelled at him and all my quiet hopes came loudly spilling out. He was dumbfounded. He had no idea he was supposed to propose, no idea I had a relationship schedule in my head, or that even though I pretended to hate romantic gestures, I still craved them. We took a long walk on the beach and talked about the state of our relationship. Looking back on it later, I realized neither of us said the thing that should have been said. His complete lack of enthusiasm toward our three-year relationship and my focus on our future instead of our present should have been indicators that it was a great time to walk away. We should have realized that our best days together had passed. But like continuing to watch a TV show years after it jumped the shark because the first season was so good, Jeff and I plodded on.

And for me, much of our first season *was* amazing. One of those times that solidified my love for Jeff for years to come happened about ten months into dating, late one night on a quiet Venice street. I had a habit of banging on the back of a car if it ignored me in the crosswalk and made the right turn right in front of me. Jeff said this was extremely dangerous because what if the person in the car is crazy or violent, or has a gun? I figured, whatever, I'm from Miami, I can handle it. On this particular night, Jeff and I had just stepped into the crosswalk when a car came whizzing by, not even acknowledging us. I slammed on the back of the car with a fulfilling whack.

The car came to a screeching halt and a very stout Italian-looking guy, shiny gold chains and all, got out and walked right toward Jeff. "What the fuck? You fuckin' touch my car?" I'm not the type of girl who will deliberately get my boyfriend into a bar fight, or cause drama and then expect someone else to clean it up, or sue Amtrak because they had a door open on a moving train even though I was the one dumb enough to try to jump through it. So when this guy blamed Jeff, it only made sense for me to jump in. "I'm the one who touched your car. Because you almost hit me in the crosswalk." The guy didn't seem to care that I had done it and was set on blaming Jeff. Jeff somehow understood this weird man code, but I was still trying to use logic.

Jeff kept pushing me behind him, shielding me from the guy. I kept walking around in front of Jeff, letting the guy know that if he was going to "fuck someone up," it should be me. I was the one who hit his car and Jeff had nothing to do with it.

Poor Jeff. He had to assess the situation, protect me (and I was making it extremely difficult by continually stepping in front of him), and at the same time protect himself. I was just trying to do the right thing, take responsibility for my own actions and keep Jeff out of it. I knew Jeff wouldn't just stand by and watch this guy beat me up because he had warned me time and time again not to hit anyone's car, but I was clearly not thinking it through.

Watching Jeff as the guy approached us was a thing of beauty. Jeff puffed up his already large frame like a lion ready to go into battle. At the same time, he calmly defused the situation with his nonescalating voice and friendly language. He was firm but not abrasive, strong but not offensive. He was able to show this guy he would put up a good fight without actually starting a fight. Jeff was everything a man should be: protective, calm, quick, smart, and levelheaded. The last time Jeff pushed me behind him I melted with admiration. You never know how someone will act until they are in the situation and I now knew Jeff was good under pressure, good in an emergency, and good at not making things worse while still holding his ground.

After about three minutes of back-and-forth Jeff had mostly resolved the conflict. It was at this time that I noticed the guy was holding something in his right hand. It wasn't brass knuckles or a knife or a gun. It was a lollypop. A little red lollypop he must have been enjoying in the car and didn't think to put down before the impromptu battle. The guy looked at us and said, "If you ever touch my car again, I'll kick your ass." That statement made no sense whatsoever. When would I ever see the guy again to have an opportunity to touch his car? I responded with, "What are you going to kick my ass with? Your lollypop?"

The guy looked down, realizing he was still holding it, and all his bravado deflated like a sad popped beach ball. Once you get caught with a lollypop you lose your scary factor. The guy walked back to his car, gold chains looking a little less shiny, and drove off.

Jeff was furious at me for several reasons but I didn't care. I wouldn't have done it any differently because I was so in love with him after that night. The experience was worth it because it allowed me to see the best in him, even if he then saw the worst in me. Those are the defining moments that are so hard to let go of, even though they are years removed from your current day-to-day relationship.

So instead of really thinking about my current relationship with Jeff, I was thinking about Jennifer and how truly happy she looked wearing that ring. It's a dangerous thing when you start comparing yourself to your friends. If the comparisons make you feel better—for instance, me loving the fact that Jeff and I were so progressive that we could be honest about our sex lives when my friends were stuck with bourgeois views—it means you are still so insecure that you need to judge your friends to build up yourself. And if the comparisons make you feel worse, it means your self-worth is tied in to how other people are living their lives. But on our three-year anniversary, I couldn't stop myself from thinking about Jennifer's boyfriend proposing to her on a rooftop or Michelle's boyfriend recently hiding her engagement ring in a Christmas ornament or Mary mischievously and romantically eloping with her boyfriend. Wasn't I as good as them? Didn't I deserve a proposal too? Wasn't I worth someone loving me and wanting to marry me?

Jeff told me he didn't quite see the point of marriage. "If we love each other, why do we need the piece of paper? Why do we have to prove it to anyone else? It's not like marriage solves anything." And of course I came back with the age-old "Well, if it doesn't matter one way or the other, then why not just get married?" That rebuttal does no one any good. To be perfectly honest, I'm not sure I knew what the point of marriage was either. I had a vague notion that it would solve all sorts of problems by ending my amorphous anxiety. I would get to wear a pretty ring, pay less for car insurance, and say things like, "Oh, my husband prefers aisle seats." (Not that I would have a chance to say that since getting Jeff on a plane was nearly impossible because he didn't like to travel with pot, and he didn't like to be anywhere without pot. And he hated going anywhere anyway.)

I was so invested in my timetable that I didn't give myself the option to not get married. I didn't ask myself if Jeff was really the one for me, or if I wanted to get married just to distract myself from the fact that my latest script didn't sell, or because although I liked to feel superior to my friends, I really wanted to be just like them. Instead of searching my own soul to find the reasons I wanted to get married to Jeff, I gave him a lot of attitude about not wanting to marry me.

After the three-year anniversary kerfuffle, I became a passive-aggressive ultimatum-giving victim. Very attractive, I know. But I would try to intercut the pouting, pathetic hostility with being a superawesome, carefree, easygoing, best girlfriend ever. Jeff was thoroughly confused.

A few weeks later we went to the suburbs of Chicago to spend Thanksgiving with his family. This was my third Thanksgiving there, and I felt very much at home in the cozy house filled with sugar cookies, crocheted blankets, and firewood.

I knew Jeff's mother well since she came out to L.A. every summer to visit him. I nicknamed her the Nicest Woman in the World. The first time I met her she hugged me and I burst into tears. I ran into another room and sobbed for a good twenty minutes. Then I pulled myself together and we all went out for Chinese food. When TNWITW hugged me I felt something that I had never felt before: unconditional love. I didn't realize how much I was starved for this feeling until I experienced it and once I did I was overwhelmed with its absence. I didn't need to prove myself to Jeff's mom at all. I didn't need to be pretty or to say anything clever or to tell her I had just sold my first reality game show. She loved Jeff, and Jeff loved me, and that was all she needed to know. She was incredibly kind, accepting, understanding, and warm. She would never call me Snausage.

Berns met her the following year and confirmed that she was in fact the Nicest Woman in the World. Susan said, "Well, then, I don't want to meet her." John tried to convince Susan that it wasn't a competition and when Susan did meet Jeff's mom, she too was rendered powerless by her sincere goodness, and they became fast friends.

Maybe it was being surrounded by such unconditional love from TNWITW and from Jeff's three wonderfully quirky aunts and stalwart uncle, but Jeff and I both let the tension of the past few weeks dissolve and we had a grand time. Once his family had all gone to bed we stayed bundled up on the couch marveling at a life without cable TV, playing cribbage, and just watching the snow fall.

The night before Thanksgiving, while we tried to battle the time difference and the air mattress and fall asleep, Jeff rolled over in bed and said, "So, how do you want to do this?" I knew that was a marriage proposal.

Because Jeff was so much heavier than me, anytime we were on a flimsy mattress his side would be much lower so I would sort of fall into him. I loved nuzzling into his chocolate-tobacco-smelling teddy bear chest and allowing his deep breaths to lull me into a relaxed, meditative state. Sometimes I even drooled on his shoulder. This was how Jeff and I were lying when he proposed. Sure, I would have liked a ring, or a grand gesture. Or him even actually saying, "Sascha, will you marry me?" But I convinced myself this was nice too. It was so "us." We didn't need to do things like other people. We didn't need the fanfare to prove our love and we didn't need the usual traditions of it seeming like he actually cared enough about me to put some effort into a proposal. If my family didn't need to say "I love you," why would my husband need to get down on one knee? All Jeff and I needed was to be snuggled in bed and for him to say, "So, how do you want to do this?" and for me to actually know him so well that I understood. That was the kind of amazing connection we had. The kind of connection that would make our marriage last forever. "This is just crazy enough to work" became a refrain I started repeating in my head, and out loud.

I didn't skip a beat and immediately started talking about the wedding plans. I was happy again and Jeff was happy that I was happy. But sadly for both of us, he fell into the trap of begrudgingly giving me what I thought I wanted.

Step 11

Plan the Divorce While You Plan the Wedding (or Choose Pavé Diamonds)

The morning after the rollover proposal, we told Jeff's family we were engaged. They were thrilled for us. His aunt and uncle, who had been married for over thirty years, had heard us talking all night through the walls and I always wondered what they thought of how the marriage proposal went down. Certainly they knew, as I did, that poetic fanfare, intricate proposals, and expensive rings didn't make a marriage. But did they worry about Jeff's lack of enthusiasm and my willingness to settle? Because those things don't make a marriage either.

I called Jennifer, Michelle, and Mary and regaled them with the story of the night before. I reiterated that Jeff and I were so perfect for each other because we were equally unromantic. Susan and John seemed distractedly happy for me but uninvolved. Berns, who had been with her boyfriend for years and philosophically didn't see the point in marriage, was at least excited to have a party to plan.

A couple of days later Jeff returned to Los Angeles. I stayed in Chicago for another week on assignment for the illustrious reality show *Who Wants to Marry My Dad?* I wonder what that flight back was like for Jeff. Was he sitting there, stunned, thinking, *Fuck, I just got engaged?* Was he excited? Was he regretting the whole half-assed thing?

While in Chicago I spent a lot of time with my soon-to-be in-laws. Jeff's mom took me to get my nails done, bought me wedding magazines, and introduced me to people as her son's fiancée. It was comforting to have someone show so much excitement that I was getting married.

Jeff made no mention of an engagement ring, and he hated shopping more than I hated beach sand in the bed, so I knew if I wanted a ring I would have to take care of it myself. While in a mall with Jeff's family that week, I wandered into a jewelry store. Not a supercheesy one, but it was in the mall nonetheless. I looked at all the diamonds glistening under the special overhead jewelry store lights that make everything look bigger and shiner. I tried on several rings, admiring my newly manicured hands, and my ring finger looked exceptionally happy enveloped in diamonds. I wondered if it seemed sad that a woman was in there all alone trying on engagement rings. The Nicest Woman in the World and Jeff's aunts were with me, but did the employees of the store wonder why the groom-to-be was not there? Or were they used to this sort of thing?

Although I had the *"this is just crazy enough to work"* line running through my head, it kept being intercepted by *"hmm, what a waste of money if I buy an engagement ring and then we get divorced."* While trying on rings, I was vaguely aware that I kept specifically picking something nontraditional. Rings with dozens of beautiful, dazzling pavé diamonds instead of one larger stone. I decided if I went with three stackable, pavé-diamond-encrusted white gold bands instead of a solitary diamond engagement ring, that would solve all problems. The rings were unique and beautiful and when worn together looked like one incredible, thick, sparkling wedding ring. If the marriage lasted, I would be happy for years to come wearing the flat, classic, pavé diamond bands. If I got divorced, I could wear the rings on my right hand and, like the commercials say, enjoy those diamonds forever. I bought my rings with my credit card. Upon my return to L.A., as agreed, Jeff paid me back for half the cost of the rings with a check. It might have been the least romantic purchase of an engagement ring in the history of courtship, but I convinced myself it was perfect by bragging to friends and family that we were such a strong couple we didn't need the usual silly traditions. Just as I convinced myself it was a good thing that we were the type of couple who could be honest with each other about how many people we had slept with. It was great that Jeff could smoke pot and play Grand Theft

Auto for hours on end without me getting upset and that I could go out with my friends, get drunk, and come home in the middle of the night with wet hair and he wouldn't be fazed. It was perfect that we were never jealous or threatened and we rarely fought. We were the couple that other couples envied.

Step 12

Get Married for a Down Payment

So if I was already thinking about divorce, then why get married? Because the train had already left the station, and there were no doors flapping open. Because after the fuss I made it felt too late to turn back now. Because planning the wedding was fun, exciting, and a great distraction from my usual life. My desire to get married was caused by a perfect storm of misguided factors: my backwards notion that being married would make me a complete person, my rigid internal clock, and, most important, the fact that I really, really wanted to own property in Los Angeles and at the rate my career was going, I would never be able to afford a place on my own.

John, a bestselling author on the subject of fiscal practicality, told Berns and me that when the time came we could either have a big, fancy wedding or a down payment. I wanted that down payment. I had this notion that, like getting married, owning a condo would soothe my anxiety about my life, my career, and living in L.A. It would provide a safe haven. A place where I could paint the walls and remove the ugly venetian blinds without worrying about getting my security deposit back. Jeff and I could afford a mortgage but we needed that chunk of money to buy. It wasn't my only reason to get married, but it was a huge plus. Why not parlay our love for each other into a home?

Once we filed for divorce and Jeff moved out and I was left to keep the condo spotless and smelling like cookies for all the open houses, I was struck with what a short-sighted idiot I was. Since we'd only lived there for two years, the market hadn't gone up that much, and between the cost of putting in the hardwood floors, scraping the cottage cheese off the ceiling, and all the initial inspections and the closing costs, we didn't make much of a profit. And because we were married and it was a wedding gift to both of us, Jeff walked off with half of the down payment.

It was like the time when I was five years old and I desperately wanted tap-dancing lessons. I convinced Susan and John I was serious about this new endeavor, so they signed me up for classes and got me the required outfits and the shoes. As I clicked and clacked throughout the tiled house day and night, they quickly realized that all I really wanted was the shoes. I wanted to wear those shiny, noise-making, patent leather beauties everywhere: to school, to Carvel, to sleep. I had no real interest in learning how to dance. I only went to one class, but the shoes I cherished for months.

Susan asked me why I hadn't just told her I wanted the shoes. It would have saved time and money. It hadn't occurred to me I could have the shoes without the lessons. And over twenty years later, it didn't occur to me I could have the condo without the marriage. I could have just asked John if I could borrow the money or saved up and tried to buy one on my own in a few more years. I could have also shelved that desire to own property and been content to rent in a city where small houses run upwards of a million dollars.

Step 13

Drive Yourself to the Doctor

About a month before the wedding I woke up with a throbbing pain coming from my mouth. I jumped up and looked in the mirror and I saw a giant pustule just left of center on my upper lip. My first thought was, *I was stung by a spider in the middle of the night. Or maybe a killer bee.* I had never seen anything like it and was horrified. I woke Jeff up. He looked at it, mildly amused by the mass on my lip since I am always so skin conscious, and went back to sleep. It was too early for him to care about anything and he clearly hadn't had his coffee and cigarettes yet so I couldn't expect him to advise or console me.

I got dressed, feebly tried to cover up the pulsating tumor with lip gloss, and went to work. The second I walked into the office people said, "What the fuck happened to your lip?" "Did you get into a fight?" "Are you okay?" "Is it contagious?" "Don't touch anything on my desk." My boss immediately sent me to her doctor.

The doctor took one look at me and said I had a very bad cold sore. I told her I had never had a cold sore before. She said the initial outbreak is usually the worst and she didn't often see it this bad in adults since most people first contract the virus and get them as kids.

The doctor said the virus had lived dormant in my body all those years and just now decided to pop out. She asked, "Are you under any new stress?" I informed her I was getting married in a month. So yes. She gave me some antiviral medication, some topical cream, and sent me on my way, saying I should be all cleared up in ten days, plenty of time before the wedding.

I got home and found Jeff still asleep. I spent the day watching Lifetime movies, chatting with Berns on the phone, and trying to forget my throbbing lip. Berns wanted to see my ailment so I took a picture and e-mailed it to her. She immediately called and advised that I show no one else and stay home. The next morning I woke up to see that the cold sore had doubled in size. The entire left side of my face was swollen and the pain was so intense I felt woozy when I stood. I needed to go back to the doctor immediately. I woke Jeff up and told him I had to go back to the doctor. He mumbled, "Okay," but didn't show any signs of getting out of bed to drive me there. I could have screamed at him and pushed him out of bed and forced him to take me, or I could have asked very nicely, but I was so hurt he didn't immediately offer that I decided to be a martyr and drive myself.

Jennifer or Michelle would have taken me in a second

but I was too embarrassed to call them. If I were single or if Jeff had been out of town I would have called. But I had a perfectly good fiancé snoring in bed and he should be the one taking me to the doctor. If I called a friend for a ride she would immediately ask, "Where's Jeff?" Then she would know that he was not such a lovable, introverted, pot-smoking teddy bear after all; that we didn't have an enviable relationship; and that he was selfish, lazy, and unsympathetic.

On my way to the doctor's, feeling like the Elephant Man, I thought about all the places Jeff wouldn't take me. The airport was off-limits because of the dense traffic near LAX. There too, I couldn't ask any of my friends for rides, because I knew full well their own significant others took them to the airport. So I always took a cab. When my car needed an occasional tune-up I always waited at the place because Jeff didn't want to have to drive there with me so early in the morning. The only instances I could ever get Jeff to drive anywhere for me were the couple of times I drank too much. One night at Sky Bar (the kind of list-only hipster place that Jeff avoided at all costs), I had one too many mojitos and pleaded with him to come collect me. I left word with the doorman to let the guy in the ratty trench coat in, and once he was through the velvet rope and inside the swanky club he found me at the pool bar chatting with my friends. I thought maybe since he was finally there he might want to look around and enjoy the place for a bit, but it was straight home for us.

During one of Susan and John's visits to L.A., Susan

took Michelle and me out for a girls' brunch. We ended up having countless Bellinis and were hammered by noon. I called Jeff and slurred to him that Michelle, Susan, and I were trashed and we couldn't possibly drive and please come pick us up. Jeff drove his car to the restaurant with John, and John drove us all home in my car. John was amused that the ladies were cackling and drunk in the middle of the day. Jeff was annoyed that he had been pulled from his morning coffee and cigarettes routine.

When I arrived at the doctor's office for my cold sore the receptionist took one look at me and got me in immediately. The doctor couldn't hide her alarm and said that my cold sore was out of hand. She gave me several shots of something directly into my lip. I passed out. When I came to, seeing concerned nurses hovering over me, I was hit with the realization that I was alone and would have to drive myself back home.

I wondered if maybe my cold sore was a sign. Maybe like the looks Ray gave me, my body knew something I didn't and was trying to tell me something. But just as the doctor said, in ten days I was healed up and ready to get married. And I did just that.

Step 14

Don't Mention the Word "Forever" at the Wedding

The minute Jeff "proposed," I stopped eating. I had a little turkey and cranberry sauce for Thanksgiving dinner and didn't even look at the mashed potatoes, apple pie, and bowls of peanut M&Ms perched on every surface. Like most brides, I was determined to be skinny for my wedding and in the three and a half months leading up to March thirteenth, I again lost that thirty pounds. Dinner became a Diet Pepsi with a wedge of lemon. Jeff was already so used to my crazy yo-yo dieting phases that he didn't pay much attention. I don't actually remember what he did pay attention to during those months. I was busy working on a terrible show for TBS and planning our small, inexpensive, yet charming wedding.

We decided to have only thirty-eight guests consisting of our closest friends and immediate family, lots of colorful cupcakes instead of a cake, and no horrendous wedding band. It was held at Michelle's beautiful little house in Studio City. She had just gotten married three months before and had an over-the-top Beverly Hills wedding with fake snow and a fairy-tale dress. In one of his rare social appearances, Jeff accompanied me to her wedding, but he was irritated because he had to wear a suit and sit next to a White Sox fan. We looked around at Michelle's lavish affair and reminded ourselves we were going in a different direction. The less money we spent on the wedding, the more money we'd have for a down payment.

On our wedding day, I wore a new, simple strapless dress of antique-white silk shantung that fell to just below my knees and had a little dip in the back hem that hit the middle of my calves. Berns and Jennifer, my maid of honor and bridesmaid respectively, wore similar dresses in currant red. Instead of a veil I put dozens of curvy white ribbons in my long wavy red hair, and one turquoise ribbon hung in the back for my something blue. I borrowed a delicate necklace of diamond vines and matching earrings from Michelle's mom and donned a simple gold band on my right pinkie that Susan had worn on a chain around her neck for as long as I could remember. This was my something old. Susan had given me the gold chain and ring at my shower, held a week before at Mary's house. I opened the box and was shocked to see Susan's necklace lying there. I had forever seen it around her neck and it meant a tremendous amount for her to pass it on to me. A tear tried to come out of my eye. Berns saw the infant tear and almost had one herself, but we willed them back in. The fact that there even was a wedding shower was already unlike us. No need to add tears of happiness to the equation.

Oddly enough, I don't remember what Jeff wore at our wedding. I remember going to buy matching red-and-gray-striped ties for his best man (Ray) and his grooms-man (his uncle). But did Jeff wear a tie? I know he wore a white button-down shirt. Did he wear his good jeans? I had to look at the pictures, which are now neatly stacked in a large IKEA box in the closet, next to the diaries and gummy bears. The pictures show him wearing black pants, a white button-down, and no tie.

The wedding was perfect. I walked down the make-shift aisle to Joe Jackson's "Is She Really Going Out with Him?"—an homage to our inherent oppositeness. Right before John and I emerged from the house to walk down the aisle I said, "I'm going to puke." "Just take a breath," John responded. Which I did. Joe Jackson sang as we made the short journey to the corner of the lawn. My old friend and officemate Owen had gotten ordained online for free, and in a matter of seconds, at the Universal Life Church. He had become a successful comedy writer and we decided to put his talents to use. He married us with a tight seven-minute set.

In true Los Angeles writer form, Owen wrote out the ceremony, including the vows Jeff and I had written, in script format, and gave me a copy after the wedding.

SASCHA AND JEFF'S WEDDING

EXT. A HOUSE IN STUDIO CITY—DAY

Officiant OWEN is on the stage with the lovely couple.

> OWEN
> Jeff and Sascha have asked me to
> perform the ceremony uniting them
> in holy matrimony. So let's start by
> figuring out how we got here today.
> Sascha moved out to Los Angeles to
> become a rich and famous writer.
> Jeff moved out to L.A. to become a
> rich and famous actor. So it seems
> almost poetic that they would meet
> while working as a waitress and
> bartender at the Improv. And what
> follows is the classic story . . . Girl
> meets Boy. Boy likes Girl. Girl likes
> Boy, but not unless he gets new
> glasses. Boy gets new glasses . . .
> Girl falls in love. Boy falls in love but
> tries to maintain independence. Girl
> gets job on *Street Smarts* and leaves
> town for weeks at a time. Longing for
> more time with Girl, Boy scraps
> independence and decides he's ready
> to move in. Girl moves to Venice even

though she hates the beach. Boy has no idea Girl is expecting to get engaged at three-year anniversary. . . . Said anniversary comes, Girl freaks out. But, on his own volition, Boy proposes on Thanksgiving weekend. And here we are today. Before we continue with the ceremony, I have to ask . . . does anyone here have any reason as to why these two should not be united? (wait a beat) Other than Jeff . . . ? (audience laughs) Then let's proceed to the vows.

JEFF

I promise to love, cherish, and tolerate Sascha . . . through countless rewrites, constant emotional turmoil, and unbelievable annoyances from her cat, Spork.

Officiant OWEN turns to SASCHA.

SASCHA

I promise to love, cherish, and not complain about . . . interminable Cubs seasons, fruitless auditions, and endless piles of plaid shirts.

> OWEN
> Jeff . . . here's Sascha's ring. Say
> something nice.

[Jeff then whispered something in my ear because we were too embarrassed to say anything nice to each other in front of guests.]

SASCHA puts a ring on JEFF's finger.

> OWEN (CONT'D.)
> Sascha . . . give it a shot.

[I whispered something unmemorable in Jeff's ear.]

JEFF puts a ring on SASCHA's finger.

> OWEN (CONT'D.)
> By the power vested in me, by the
> power of the Internet, I now
> pronounce you married.

A glass is placed under JEFF's foot. JEFF breaks the glass. The crowd shouts, "Mazel Tov."

> OWEN (CONT'D.)
> You may now kiss the bride.

SASCHA and JEFF kiss.

Our vows were extremely personal, in that they were about us and solely us, but nowhere did we say anything about "till death do us part" or use words like "eternal" and "forever." Jeff and I discussed that point beforehand and decided that to put that much pressure on a marriage would surely make it destined for failure. Maybe that was why there was so much divorce: because people say "forever," then feel trapped, and then have to escape. So we thought, in our "crazy enough to work" mindset, that by eliminating all promises of forever, we might just end up together forever. We were wrong.

Saying "forever" certainly doesn't mean you can necessarily pull it off. But by not saying it, we were giving ourselves a huge out. Like when someone asks you to help them move and you say, "I'll try." That really means, "Under no circumstances will I be waking up at seven a.m. to help lug your furniture around town." By not ever really expecting to be together for the rest of our lives, we were setting ourselves up for a short-term marriage.

After the stand-up comedy ceremony, I ate for the first time in months. The money we did spend on our reception went mostly toward an amazing chef and scrumptious dinner. We dined and drank. Everyone laughed when Ray raised a glass and toasted us with "To the best five years of your life." He was off by quite a bit.

I made a toast about how our wedding was so small because we only wanted to invite the people closest to us. The ones we were certain we would be speaking to in ten years. Susan later pointed out how ironic it was that the one person I would certainly not be speaking to in ten years was my husband.

For our wedding night, Jeff and I had booked a suite at a nice hotel near Venice. But after the wedding, we were so exhausted we just wanted to go home and crawl into our own bed. Berns called the hotel for us and, using her persuasive charms, convinced them not to charge us even though we were canceling far less than twenty-four hours in advance. All our friends went home. Our families went back to their hotels. And by midnight, Jeff and I were curled up in bed together. I felt truly at peace resting on his belly. We were so happy together at home, we didn't want to be anywhere else, not even a place with room service and a Jacuzzi. We both commented on how this was a very good sign for our marriage. We didn't need all the trimmings to be content. We just needed each other.

Step 15

Compromise to the Point That Both Parties Are Unhappy

After I checked "getting married" off the invisible list in my head, wrote all the thank-you notes, and enjoyed our very short honeymoon at the Four Seasons in Santa Barbara, I moved right on to the next item: buying a condo. I found a Realtor and a loan officer and started looking at places. We couldn't afford a place in Venice, which I hated anyway, and Jeff hated Hollywood. So we bought a condo in a place we both hated: Sherman Oaks.

Sherman Oaks is in the San Fernando Valley, just north of the mountains that loom over Los Angeles. There are some good things about the Valley. There is always plenty of parking, it is less expensive, and there is a car wash on every block. But mostly there are bad things. It's sweltering, even for someone who grew up in Miami Beach; it has no aesthetic character; and during rush hour it can take an hour to drive the five miles over the hill into L.A.

After looking at several vaguely depressing places in the Valley, we stumbled upon a two-bedroom, two-bath, 950-square-foot condo on a cul-de-sac. The giant, always bumper-to-bumper 405 freeway was what was causing the street to dead-end, but it was hidden behind a row of cleverly placed trees and the street was surprisingly quiet. Although there were no hipster bars, good restaurants, museums, or furry little ducklings near us, there was a Target a mile up the road.

Jeff once told me he had briefly lived with a girl in Chicago and it was such a disaster he would spend his nights wandering through the aisles of the nearby Target just to get away from her. In our final year of marriage when I would run in there to get lightbulbs or sports bras or kitty litter, and I would end up slowly perusing the pajamas section and the office supplies section, I wondered if I was just stalling my return home.

As first-time buyers Jeff and I made a few mistakes. We bought in the nicest building, which wasn't that nice, on an unappealing block. And we bought the nicest unit in a building that was dilapidated. Then we overimproved the unit with beautiful hardwood floors, smooth ceilings, and a trellis on the balcony. I now know to buy the worst place in the best location. Better for resale value.

When we moved in a few months after the wedding we felt a real sense of pride. Sure, Susan and John had sprung for the down payment, but Jeff and I were paying the mortgage. We walked around the place opening cabinets, peering in closets, and surveying the balcony, which we called "the back forty," saying things like, "We own this closet," "We own this wall," and "We own this toilet." It was an exciting realization. We hired one of Jeff's buddies to paint the condo and we paid him in pot. It took him months to finish, because he was always stoned, but I didn't mind. I was so happy with the pale blue in the living room, the ruby red in the kitchen, the forest green in the bedroom, and the merlot purple in my office that I didn't dwell on the delay. The painter sort of became a part of our little family and would often help me carry in groceries, throw Spork a toy mouse, and take breaks to watch Jeff play Grand Theft Auto.

As the months wore on, Jeff spent more and more time in his chair smoking pot and I spent more and more time gallivanting with my friends. We became alienated from each other and the condo.

I hated pulling into the garage under the building, seeing the piles of junk stacked next to the Dumpsters, noticing the sign that the building elevator was still out of order, and running into one of the five sons, ages eighteen to forty, of the married couple that lived above us, shadowboxing amid the cars. Their dad used to be a boxer and a trainer. One of the middle sons was insanely sexy and dirty, like Brad Pitt in *Thelma & Louise*, and made me feel both uncomfortable and excited.

Once inside the apartment, surrounded by our deep-jewel-toned walls and our cheery furniture, I felt great. But the drive up to the place always made me feel I had made a mistake. If I felt alienated from friends when I lived in Venice, Sherman Oaks was like living on Mars. As I passed the sad, empty batting cages, the lonely box store, and the struggling pizza place with its three-year-old Grand Opening sign, my stomach sank. I shouldn't have been in such a hurry to own property. Then I would quickly remind myself that this is good for our credit. Good to pay a mortgage instead of rent. A good starter home for five years and then we would be ready to move somewhere a bit nicer.

I think Jeff never wanted to leave his chair because walking outside would be a reminder he was no longer in Venice. I convinced myself I loved Sherman Oaks because it was my idea to move there, and Jeff convinced himself he loved it because it was good for his financial future. The truth was, we both hated it.

After the divorce, Jeff admitted that he had decided moving to the Valley would be the last thing he ever did for me. Once I heard him say that, I looked back on our two years there and everything became clearer. He resented me for wanting to get married and for ripping him away from the beach, so he withdrew from me and made me the enemy. Deciding in month three of a marriage that you are done doing anything for your spouse is a quiet way of poisoning the relationship. Like sprinkling arsenic on someone's English muffin every morning, it might take a while, but eventually she will get sick and die.

Step 16

Keep Your Belongings Separate

When Jeff and I first moved in together, we didn't combine any of our possessions. We had different dresser drawers and closet space, of course, but we took it much further than most couples. Everything was separate. I had a bookshelf for my books; he had one for his books. We even kept our CDs on different racks. Jeff joked that my music was so god-awful that he didn't want it mingling side by side with his music. He wouldn't put my *Best of Bon Jovi* anywhere near his Foo Fighters. It was fine by me since I was so particular about how I arranged my things anyway.

When we moved from our little place on the canals to the condo in Sherman Oaks, we still kept everything separate. We made the joke that this way, there would be no arguments about whose book was whose when we got a divorce.

It wasn't just material goods; we didn't really combine

anything. I kept my last name. We never signed up for a family plan for our cell phones or joined the same gym. We never combined income or shared credit cards, and we maintained different bank accounts. Although we stood in front of our closest friends and family and were legally joined together in a state of matrimony, we never really joined together.

I know lots of happily married people with different last names, bank accounts, and cell phone providers, but if when adding all the separates up, you find that there is no togetherness, it's a bad sign. One I didn't register until it was way too late.

Step 17

Include Your Spouse in a Performance Where You Read Off Your List of Sexual Partners

A few years into my relationship with Jeff, my friend Dave created a comedy show called *Mortified*, where people read from their old diaries with ironic self-awareness to an audience of people laughing so hard they are either crying or peeing. I had been a part of *Mortified* from its inception, and in planning my next appearance I mentioned to Dave that I had kept a list of all the guys I had ever slept with.

I started the list while on a plane returning home from a summer studying playwriting in Dublin, between my sophomore and junior years of college. I was looking out the window, seeing nothing but sky and ocean, feeling European and introspective, and writing in my diary, when I wondered if maybe there was a correlation between the meaning of life and all the guys I had chosen to sleep with. The most recent guy was an Irish plumber I met in a bar, who looked like Ethan Hawke and enjoyed making himself cry on cue. We had a delightful three-week fling and when it was time for me to return to America he started sobbing, saying he thought we were going to be together forever. I told Susan this over the phone and she said, "Well, did you sleep with him?" And I said yes, and she responded, "No wonder he thought you were going to be together. People in Ireland don't go running around having casual sex."

So I made a list. Then I wrote the initials of all the guys in a row and scrambled around all the letters trying to spell out a word, any word that would be some sort of a sign or message. There was nothing. Too many consonants.

Once I had started the list, I kept it updated over the years. Beyond just names, I included a key code at the bottom. Hearts next to the name meant I thought I was in love, a check meant he was good in bed, a hat meant he was uncircumcised. Dave thought this list not only exemplified my need to structure what is inherently unstructured but was comedy gold and would make for a fantastic *Mortified* segment.

He blew up the list at Kinko's and I stood in front of an audience in an L.A. theater going down the list, explaining my key code and my need to document everything. I ended the bit by saying my list was now officially closed because I had gotten married to the last guy on the list and he had both a heart and two checks next to his name. The audience would always let out a collective, "Awwww."

Then I would reveal that not only is my husband confident enough for me to be onstage telling the world how many people I have slept with, but he is so confident, he is actually the guy holding the list. On that cue Jeff would step out from behind the giant list.

The audience gasped.

Most of my girlfriends were still lying about how many guys they had slept with and were in denial about their long-term boyfriends or husbands watching porn or fantasizing about others during sex. And most of my guy friends were shocked that not only could Jeff handle my sex list, but he thought it was funny. In our eyes, this made us the coolest, most confident, well-adjusted, best couple ever.

Until it didn't.

Feeling so insecure that you read private letters, cheat, have to go to therapy to cope, and lie to your therapist about it all is all sorts of bad. But being so void of feelings about your partner that you have no semblance of jealously isn't any better. I should have been devastated when Jeff told me he thought about other girls when his dick was in my mouth. He should have told me to fuck off when I told him I wanted to go with someone else to the Playboy Mansion and asked him to wait for me when I got home so I could put my repressed sexual desires onto him. I mean really, if not cheating on him that night was so difficult, I had no business being with him in the first place.

Jeff and I didn't establish a long-lasting bond by being honest and apathetic. We established that neither of us cared enough about the other to feel at least a little bit possessive. When I was with Adam I was so sick of fearing Housna that I went too far in the other direction and had no problem with Jeff's ex-girlfriend hanging around, his flirting at the bar to get more tips, or him thinking of me as just a hole from time to time. Jeff and I had sex consistently up to the end of our marriage, but it wasn't full of passion and romance. Instead it became sex by numbers. Put red there. Green here. Brown there. Voilà! Our sex life was a still life of an apple.

One night we were having sex and Jeff's favorite pre-prime-time show, *Jeopardy*, was on in the background. Jeff usually watched it while sitting in his chair, clicking a pen as if it was the contestant button, practicing for when he got on the show. (He auditioned and failed every year.) On this rare night we were actually in Vegas, having hot hotel sex on the bed. While we were literally in the middle of intercourse Jeff yelled out, "What is Vermont?" He got it right. He was so engrossed in the show and so disinterested in the sex that he didn't even realize he said the answer out loud. I thought it was hysterical! "What is Vermont?" became one of our favorite stories to tell and phrases to say. Instead of being horrified that we were both so disconnected, we embraced that it was normal and natural for couples to become bored with each other in bed.

But although fading fervor is normal, there also has to be a little jealously, a little insecurity, and a little possessiveness. A little anger that Vermont and Alex Trebek were more tantalizing than my naked body.

Step 18

Marry an Actor

When Jeff and I met, we needed each other for support and encouragement and a sense of stability in a crazy, scary town that will eat your soul and then puke it up because it has too many calories. We understood each other's endless struggle to find work, to convince agents to call us back, and to get producers to remember our names. We both understood that our careers had to come first and we understood that the daily ups and downs of getting that audition or meeting, and then finding out you didn't get the job, were going to take a toll on our moods and couldn't be taken personally by the other. Luckily, since Jeff was an actor and I was a writer, we were never competing with each other. Jeff was unwaveringly supportive. One of the reasons I fell in love with him was because I needed him for self-preservation. He helped me safely forge my way through the L.A. landscape of collagen, designer bags, and rejection without losing my mind or sight of my writing plans.

When I moved to L.A., Susan told me I had to call her lifelong friend, Hollywood icon and all-around curmudgeonly charmer Buck Henry. We formed our own friendship and when I told Buck that I was marrying Jeff, he said one of two things would happen: Jeff would never succeed as an actor and I would resent his constant struggles and feelings of inadequacy and leave him. Or he would succeed and leave me for someone younger and skinnier. Either way, it would not end well. Buck, as always, was right, but not for the reasons he half-jokingly predicted. For one, if Jeff was going to leave me for anyone, it wouldn't be for younger or skinnier, it would be for a girl that smoked Kamel Reds, ate corned beef, and understood the beauty of a grand slam. And I never resented Jeff for his career struggles. It was actually *his* eventual resentment of them that contributed to our demise.

About a year into dating, I left the Improv and got a job at the Palm, a high-end steak house. I was told by one of the managers that I would make so much money in tips that "if I saw a twenty lying on the floor, I wouldn't even stop to pick it up." This turned out to be egregiously untrue. Jeff was still working at the Improv and completely fed up with bartending, but it really was the best employment for a struggling actor. I had been waitressing on and off since high school, and although it wasn't as easy as my stint as a nude model for painters, as impressive as my summer interning for famed trial lawyer Roy Black, or as exciting as my year as an assistant to a fancy executive producer on *The Late Late Show*, it was part-time. This allowed me plenty of time to write, plus the work was relatively fun and paid the bills.

One night at the Palm I snapped. It wasn't overly dramatic, but it was a defining moment. I was standing there marrying ketchups after the dinner rush. (For those of you who have never worked in the restaurant industry, marrying ketchups is when you take all the half-filled bottles and combine them, so they look full and new and pretty for the next day's customers. Don't think too hard about the unsanitary implications of this, because unless you're getting ketchup out of a single serving packet, you too have used married condiments.)

I was standing there, minding my own side-working business, and all of a sudden something died inside me. Or maybe it came to life, because I realized I could not waitress for one second more. I could never fold napkins, tell people the specials, put the dressing on the side, or marry ketchup again. I had to find another way to support my not yet blossomed writing career.

I put the unmarried bottles down, walked over to the manager, and said, "Do you need my two weeks' notice? Because I can't do this anymore." He saw the insane resolve in my eyes and wisely said, "No problem. You can go home now." I never waitressed again. Jeff was proud that I once again had done what I said I would do and escaped from the sometimes excruciating world of the food service industry. He continued to bartend, which ate into his soul one little bite at a time.

The day after my divorce from the ketchups, I called a friend who had also escaped from the Improv and was now working in reality television. He invited me to a party and told me there might be some good contacts and maybe I could somehow score myself a job. Jeff, of course, didn't want to come to the party so I put on some lip gloss and went without him. The party was in Santa Monica, in a large courtyard filled with people drinking vodka and cranberry in red plastic cups. There were too many people crammed into one space for easy mingling so instead of being coy and waiting for someone to talk to me, like me, ask me what I was up to, and then offer me employment, I decided to take a different approach. I slowly made my way to the middle of the large, crowded apartment building courtyard and yelled, "I need a job! Who is going to hire me?" Two guys in the corner, gay and wearing popped collars, called me over. They needed casting assistants on *Big Brother* and someone with my outgoing personality was perfect! That started my reality show career.

I would take a job for a few months and save up money, then write for a few months, then take another reality TV job. Jeff started getting the occasional part: a toy store employee, a cop, a medical examiner. And things seemed good.

A year after our wedding, I got my first long-term writing job, at MTV. For freelancers long-term means seven months. I was elated. I got to go to MTV every day, sit in a big office, and write stuff. The people I worked with were likable and fun and didn't take themselves too seriously. We weren't curing cancer, after all. We were making television for twelve-year-olds. One night, as everyone was packing up, a producer on the show casually asked me, "Are you unhappy at home?" Without a second thought I said, "No, why?" "Because you're always the last to leave." She smiled to let me know she was kidding and she waved good-bye and walked down the hall.

Wow. I *was* always the last to leave. Was it because I was so thrilled to finally be a professional writer that I never wanted to leave my desk? Or was it because I was avoiding going from a happy environment surrounded by energetic, cheery people to a sad condo with a stoned lump sitting on a La-Z-Boy chair?

I don't know if Jeff became more depressed that year because his parts were few and far between, or if my satisfaction at work made me happier and made me notice how miserable he was and had always been. It seemed my career was finally consistently on an upswing and his was stuck at the bar. Buck's words rang in my ear.

Marrying a writer certainly has its downsides. One is that you can always fall prey to becoming material. But marrying an actor, especially a good one, is daunting because you never know when they are, well, acting. The few times Jeff would go out with me into the world, he was so much fun. I would look over at him elegantly lighting someone's cigarette, making a joke, or telling an amusing self-deprecating audition story and it seemed like he was having a blast being social and getting to know my friends and wearing a button-down. When it seemed he was enjoying himself, it made my night doubly fun. Then, once the evening was over, we would get into the car and I would excitedly turn to him and say, "See, wasn't that fun?" His face would drop, his shoulders would relax, and he would say, "Nope. Not fun."

"But it seemed like you were having a good time."

"I was acting."

For the rest of the car ride home I would be crushed. What I thought was a fun night out with my husband was in fact just another time he was putting on a show. He did it so well that sometimes I wondered, *Maybe he really is having fun. Maybe he's just saying he's not to punish me for something, to make me feel like I don't even know the real him.* I wasn't sure which was worse, him pretending to have fun and then dropping the character the second we were alone or him having fun but telling me he didn't, to maintain some sort of control.

A few days after I told Jeff I wanted a divorce, we had a dinner with my entertainment lawyer and his wife scheduled. As always, our careers came first and to help me out Jeff said he would still come with me to the dinner, and he would be his usual charming, gracious self. He wore his good jeans, a green T-shirt that made his big hazel eyes pop, and a madras jacket he'd bought for audition purposes. I fell in love with him all over again at that dinner, watching him eat naan and tikka masala. He was smart, adorable, and so supportive. For a minute I thought, *I don't want a divorce. I want to work this out. I want to save what we once had.* When we got in the car, I turned to him and said, "That was weirdly kind of fun." He responded, "Just acting."

As we were filling out our divorce papers at We the People—a great, easy place for noncontesting people to file for divorce—I started telling Jeff some story and he said, "We aren't married anymore. I don't have to feign interest." It was one last dagger. Not only was he just acting when he seemed to be having fun with me in public, he was doing the same when I was talking to him in private. There was nothing left.

Step 19

Cling to Distractions

Jeff and I were always fans of television. And because we were both working in television, or trying to, we had a great excuse for watching a lot of it. We had to keep up with the trends, the actors, the names in the credits. When we moved in together, we had two TVs of equal size and quality. His went in the living room, mine in the bedroom. We each watched the programs we enjoyed, sometimes together, sometimes in different rooms. TV was a part of our life. Then Ruby arrived and TV became our whole life.

With the money we got from Jeff's family as a wedding gift, we decided to treat ourselves to a giant, high-definition flat-screen plasma TV. I always liked the name Ruby and when I was little I wished that was my name. Ruby Rothchild. It had a nice ring to it. Trashy meets aristocratic. In my mind, there was no way anyone could have made the leap from Ruby to Sausage.

When our TV arrived in that giant box and Jeff and I opened it with loving care, we felt it was our baby.

"I want to name her Ruby," I said.

He looked down at the windshield-size, light-as-a-feather beauty. "Ruby has your eyes."

Jeff sat in his chair and smoked pot. I sat on my couch and constantly did my nails. And we watched Ruby together. Hours upon hours of TV watching. The next two years became a blur of previous seasons of *Amazing Race*, *Deadwood*, and *Lost*. One summer we watched so much *Alias* that Spork actually learned how to meow to the opening song. Between TiVo, Netflix, and what was currently on, we had endless entertainment: *Boston Legal*, *South Park*, *Six Feet Under*. Of course Jeff ordered the Bears and Cubs package so he could see every game on Ruby's beautiful crisp screen.

It was as though Jeff and I never needed to say another word to each other, because we were now married, and because we now had Ruby. She was the one thing that brought us together. Not that close together, since his chair was a good foot from my couch, but together enough to chat about bad guest stars, good cold opens, and our hatred of Randy Newman theme songs.

Watching procedurals with Jeff was sometimes trying because, based on the success of the guest-starring actors, he always deduced immediately who did it. *Without a Trace* or *CSI* or *NYPD Blue* would be on and in the first scene when the mailman of the victim would be talking to the police, Jeff would say, "He did it."

"But how do you know?"

"Because I was just at an audition with him and I know he only takes big guest spots."

Jeff was always right.

At this point I was getting consistent writing jobs, had learned to talk myself off of rewrite ledges, and didn't need Jeff for self-preservation anymore. He had learned to push himself as an actor and didn't need me for encouragement and support anymore. So although there was still general contentment between us there was no more need and because we had confused need with love, there wasn't much to fill up the space, except for Ruby.

Our lawyer friends who lived in Altadena gave us a hot-air balloon ride for a wedding present. I had always wanted to go on a hot air balloon ride so I was excited. Jeff was, well, Jeff. I used thousands of my travel rewards points for a hotel room in San Diego and made a reservation with the balloon people. Jeff took enough pot to keep him satiated for an overnight trip and we made the two-hour drive down to San Diego. We were instructed to meet the balloon people at a Ralph's grocery store parking lot and were then herded into a bus with an elderly Japanese couple, a Canadian father-and-daughter pair, and two single middle-aged women. We drove around in this bus with the other balloon-goers for about an hour until we were told the winds were just right, and a takeoff location had been chosen. We arrived, me already nauseous, Jeff not stoned anymore, at a patch of dirt off the freeway. This was not what I had in mind.

Once in the balloon, which was really just a giant RE/MAX advertisement, we floated above McMansions, strip malls, and depressing suburban compounds. The pilot pointed out the new Blockbuster and Washington Mutual that had been added to the Starbucks and Curves gym complex. We had somehow gotten stuck on a horrible suburban sprawl real estate tour when we thought we would be gliding over sun-kissed shores, hypnotic waves, and endless beaches. Instead of seeing majestic whales jumping out of the Pacific Ocean, we saw yippy dogs barking at us from their invisible-electric-fenced-in lawns.

Jeff and I bonded over this appalling forty-five–minute balloon ride, giggling on the bus back to the Ralph's and laughing all the way to our hotel room. But once in the hotel room we sat there staring at the small TV. We both felt the pressure of a night together, without Ruby, closing in on us. Luckily, Jeff got a call from his agent about an audition the following day. We both leaped up immediately, using that as a great excuse to bail on the room and our minivacation and drive back to Los Angeles immediately. We were home two hours later, both relieved to be perched in our usual spots in front of the warm glow of Ruby's screen.

On a Saturday night soon after my realization that I didn't want Jeff at my thirtieth birthday party, he and I were watching *Match Point*, Woody Allen's movie about passion, marriage, and murder. Toward the end of the movie Jeff pressed pause, turned to me, and said earnestly, "If you ever want a divorce just ask. No problem. But please, don't kill me." I laughed and at the same time felt a deep pang of loneliness. He knew me so well. While watching Jonathan Rhys Meyers get away with murder I was in fact thinking, *I could just kill Jeff.* In a warped way it seemed a better solution. Instead of becoming a coldhearted, baggage-laden divorcée, I would be a grief-stricken, mysterious widow. Assuming I didn't get caught, of course.

And how could I want to divorce a man who not only knew what I was thinking, but also had the sense of humor to joke about me murdering him? But watching Jeff rock in his chair and take another hit off his pipe, I became certain that knowing someone doesn't mean you should be married to him or her. Sometimes truly knowing someone makes you see you shouldn't.

Step 20

Call Your First Love

Billy sat behind me in biology class in tenth grade. He had transferred to my school, Beach High, after ninth grade so this was the first class we had together. He was very tall and lean with olive skin, light brown eyes, and black hair. He was the most beautiful thing I had ever seen and strikingly resembled male supermodel Marcus Schenkenberg. His hands were proportionate to his height, which means they were big, and they were smooth, hairless, and strong from playing basketball and football. He had a few rugged calluses from lifting weights, but the rest of his Brazilian skin was flawless, and the skin covering his protruding thumb muscle felt like moist cake. Billy barely said a word in class. He was the tall, dark, handsome, silent, brooding type.

We started flirting by passing notes. He always wrote in all capital letters and was a man of few words even on paper. A couple weeks of eating lunch together on the grassy area near the flagpole led to nightly phone calls, which then led to us going out. He was the type of teenage boy who trusted no one, talked to no one, and felt humans were basically evil and the human condition a pit of despair. So when Billy opened up to me, it made me feel like the most important person in the world.

It's like I always say about the whole Jesus Christ thing. If he loves everyone, no matter what, then why is his love worth anything? I never understood that. If a teacher gives everyone in class an A, then the A loses its value. When a stripper tells every customer her "real" name because it makes each customer feel special, it isn't special at all but just a manipulation. (Not to mention that "real" name is just a second fake name.) And men fall for this because they desperately need to believe a superhot half-naked chick wants them. Just like people desperately need to feel loved by someone, even if it's love from a biblical character who inherently loves all creatures. I don't want to be loved by someone who loves everyone. I want to be loved by someone who loves no one, because that makes the love special.

When Billy, who was sought after by most of the girls in my high school, chose to love me, it meant something. I fell in love with him and felt it so deeply in my teenage soul that I was certain I would die for him or die without him. And no adult was going to convince me that my fifteen-year-old emotions weren't real. In a way, they were the most real emotions I have ever had because I never questioned them for a minute. Like the little ducklings on the canals who follow around the first thing they see when they are born, which is usually and hopefully the mama duck, I was imprinted by Billy's love. No matter what love ever came after, that first unanalyzed love would always be the one I was chasing.

When we were in tenth grade Billy's parents were in the middle of a messy divorce, so every few months he would pull away, telling me he had too much to deal with. The first time he broke up with me was in a note he passed to me in biology. It read, I'M SORRY. I CAN'T HANDLE THIS RIGHT NOW. A month later, which is years in teenage time, I was still inconsolable. Jennifer and I usually went through crushes like Carnation Instant Breakfast packets so when I couldn't shake the Billy heartbreak she said, "Wow. You really love him." I really did. I moped around, wrote about him in my diary, and amazingly even lost my appetite. We got back together a week later when he said letting me go wasn't helping, but only hurting his already tumultuous world.

Billy didn't have his license yet, even though he was sixteen. He figured that there was no point in getting one since he didn't have a car to drive anyway. So I would take John's Saab out with only a learner's permit (which you could get at fifteen), risking everything, just so I could go see Billy at the basketball court or pick him up for a movie or go over to his house even if for only five minutes, after just having seen him all day in school. It never occurred to me John might be looking at the mileage to see if I was taking the car without permission, as some parents do.

But since my parents aren't like other parents, it never occurred to them to look. After a year of illegal solo driving I turned sixteen, got my real license, and then Billy and I were inseparable.

To punish his overbearing father Billy stopped playing varsity basketball and football and started spending more and more time at my house. John enjoyed watching sports with him and Susan thought he was a lovely boy who was always helpful, friendly, and quiet—a nice change from our family members. Billy was invited along on all vacations and really became part of the family. When Susan and John almost died on a white-water rafting trip down the Colorado River, Billy was there by my side as Berns, Chauncey, and I tried not to cry.

At the beginning of our junior year, one afternoon in my princess canopy bed, I took Billy's virginity. He often obsessed about how he did not take mine. He would sit in the chair in the corner of my bedroom and sulk. I would reassure him that it didn't matter that I had slept with someone before him and I would slowly bring him out of his brooding funk.

In our senior year, Billy's mother moved in with her new boyfriend and his father had a meltdown, so Billy moved in with us. Just like Dylan and Brenda on *Beverly Hills, 90210*. When Billy first moved in he was supposed to live in the guesthouse off the garage, above John's office. By week three we dropped the façade and he just slept in my room. This made John uncomfortable for a minute, as it should have. His teenage daughter was sleeping with her boyfriend down the hall from him every night. Susan, in all her antiestablishment wisdom, pointed out, "Who are we to stop them from having sex?" Susan always said she would rather I had sex safely in my room than in a car somewhere. She had a point and John gave in. So Billy stayed in the canopy. But just for fun we also sometimes had sex in the car.

Living together made an already intense first love even more heightened. When Susan and John would go away on their many trips, which included leaving for entire summers, Billy and I had the most fun. But unlike many teens, we didn't have fun partying or drag racing or being self-destructive; instead we enjoyed a domesticated life of going to the grocery store, cooking dinners together, feeding the gaggle of cats, and skinny-dipping under the moon in the giant hedge-lined pool. We were the lord and lady of the manor and felt like newlyweds. That last summer before we each left for a different college was my happiest time. And like the droves of first loves before us we were convinced we would make it through the long distance.

Billy left first. He was off to Florida State University. We woke up at five a.m. and I walked him outside where his buddies and their packed truck waited in my driveway. We hugged good-bye and with promises of undying love and constant visits, he got in the truck and vanished into the still dark morning. A week later I flew to Boston. Billy's absence was suffocating, and the daily phone calls just made things more unbearable. By Thanksgiving break we had broken up. We both agreed that we were too young to not take advantage of the college experience, but it was Billy who officially called it quits. Hootie and the Blowfish's first album was the soundtrack to my heartbreak. (Surprisingly that wasn't one of the CDs Jeff would later chide me for owning.)

I threw myself into my studies, I ate a lot of frozen yogurt, and I pined. I wrote pages and pages of pathetic diary entries and short stories about Billy. This is one of my most self-indulgent entries, written in third person:

The girl sat pensively listening to the light rain and thinking about him. Where was he right now? she wondered. Kissing someone else, perhaps. The CD just stopped. The song is over. The love is not over. Will it ever be? Am I pathetic? the girl thought. There has got to be another one out there. Another love. What if there is only one? She will be unfulfilled forever. A's make parents proud and get you invited to awards ceremonies but they don't cuddle with you at night. They don't scratch your back when there is a hard-to-reach itch. They don't hug you when you cry. What good are they?

The first date I went on after Billy and I broke up was with a guy who lived in my dorm. We went to see *The Next Karate Kid* and ended up at TGI Friday's, where I ordered hot chocolate with whipped cream. Things were going well until European history came up and he said, "I don't see the big deal about the Holocaust. Why are Jews still complaining? I mean, it happened, like, fifty years ago." Growing up in Miami Beach I was accustomed to many things, but anti-Semitism was not one of them.

I had many failed romances over the next couple of years. One with my awkward but brilliant RA who taught me to play chess. He had never kissed a girl before and I thought by helping him through the bases, I was doing him a service. Instead I gave him mixed messages, broke his heart, and drove him to never want to speak to me again. Then I met an old friend of Chauncey's, a weird Russian guy also named Sascha. He would wake up in the mornings and pretend to do tai chi. He fancied himself a mystic and said things like, "You can enter my circle or exit my circle, but you can't break my circle." Then I had a brief and exciting fling with a guy in SHARP, Skinheads Against Racial Prejudice. He would go out into the night, shaved head, crude tattoos, and Doc Martens blazing, and beat up neo-Nazi skinheads with a cue ball in a sock. Very sexy to a goth Jewish girl looking for drama. But he fell off my radar and last I heard he was in jail for inciting a riot. After such bad luck with men, I tried my hand at women and started hanging out with a bisexual girl who listened to a lot of Henry Rollins and whose pet ferret would crawl all over us in bed while we fooled around. She was a lot of fun but ultimately it didn't work out because neither of us was actually gay.

No matter whom I was dating, I was holding on to

Billy and the idea that he and I were meant to be together. And then, in that moment under the train when I thought I was going to die, I thought of him. He flashed before my eyes. His brooding stare. His smooth skin. The way he slept with one of his hands always resting on my head. I reasoned that if I thought about him when I thought I was going to die, it must mean true love. And if I loved him still, he must love me still. That was the way true love worked in my head.

I had Jennifer call him when I was in the hospital hooked up to IVs and monitors to tell him in the most theatrical way possible that I might die and I wanted him to know I still loved him.

I hadn't seen Billy since Christmas break our freshman year, when it was clear we were not getting back together. Now it was exactly two years later. I was back in Miami Beach three weeks after the accident, stuck in the make-shift bed in the library, and Billy was on his way over. Berns tried to make me look pretty although I still sort of looked like I had been hit by a train. She fluffed the pillows around me. Sprayed some perfume on my neck, and fixed my unwashed hair. My body trembled and my teeth chattered with nervous anticipation. I could see the headlights of Billy's car as it pulled up into the driveway and I held my breath as he walked into the house he once lived in.

Berns met him at the door and told him I was in the library. I saw his tall, lean form linger in the door frame for a second, and then he gently sat next to me on the bed. After much staring at each other in wonderment, we talked about everything: his redneck roommate, my comedy troupe, his computer lab job, my playwriting classes. It was like those two years apart didn't exist. After a few hours of catching up he softly kissed me on the lips and left me with the distinct feeling our time would come again.

When I recovered and returned to college, I continued to pine for Billy. Once I started dating Adam in my senior year, I pined for them both. Then, in my last month of senior year, while Adam was off in Morocco not calling me and not promising me anything, Billy called and said, "I love you. I have always loved you. And now that college is almost over we need to do something about it." He flew to Boston to spend a week with me and in that week we planned on figuring out if we should spend the rest of our lives together. Were we still really in love? Or were we in love with the memories of being in love?

After the initial excitement was out of the way, which took about five hours, we learned that although we both would always be an important part of each other's lives, we were in fact not in love. Now that nothing stood in our way, spending time together was just really boring. At the end of his visit, we cried together in the shower, grieved over the closure of our intense first love, and I drove him to Logan Airport in the Saab John let me take to college senior year. It was very fitting to be in that car together once again.

Billy and I kept in touch over the years, e-mailing or

calling every now and again. He moved to Tampa after college and sometimes he would say he still loved me and he was going to come to Los Angeles to win me back. But I knew he would never come. And sometimes when things weren't going well for me, I would think of him and for a brief moment decide he was the answer.

Jeff and I had been together for almost a year when one morning at six thirty, my phone rang. I was in bed alone since this was one of Jeff's nights off. It was Billy, calling from Tampa, to make sure I was alive and safe. I had no idea what he was talking about, so he told me to turn on the news. America was under attack. It was September 11, 2001. I immediately called Susan and John in Miami and learned that Berns was safe in New York. Then I called Billy back and we stayed on the phone for a long time. We said nothing, just watched the news. I called Jeff several times that morning but he never answered. He slept well into the afternoon, ignoring his ringing phone. And while other couples were drawn together to help cope with the tragedy, Jeff and I never connected that day. He didn't want to drive to my place and I didn't want to drive to his. Although I hadn't seen Billy since our senior year of college and he was two thousand miles away, that day I felt much closer to him than to Jeff.

Once I understood I didn't want Jeff at my thirtieth birthday party, I called Billy and told him I was confused and unhappy and that I had made a mistake getting married. He listened with concern and told me he too was unhappy in his four-year relationship. We kept in touch more over the next few months than we had in years. I in no way left Jeff for Billy, but once I knew I was going to leave Jeff, Billy again became a big part of my life. For me, reconnecting with my old flame was a sure sign that my current fire was dying out.

Step 21

Buy New Fangs and Do Cocaine Every Sunday

I'm convinced that the reason I didn't get into Yale, John's alma mater, was because of the weird vampire essay I sent with my application. It could have been because my SAT score wasn't Ivy League high, but I prefer to think it was the walking dead. My interest in vampires started when I read *Dracula*. Then, when I got my eleven-year-old hands on *Interview with a Vampire*, my interest turned into obsession. Every night I fantasized a vampire would come crawling through my window, grab my delicate neck, and shove his fangs into my skin. I would crumble into his evil strength and he would pick up my thin body with ease and carry me off to a world of sex, power, and fabulous black clothes.

To me, a post-Sausage prepubescent girl, vampires were perfection. They represented grace, strength, independence, immortality, and beauty, and most important, vampires are never fat. I thought becoming one was my shoo-in to an eternity of thinness.

At Boston College, feeling unmoved by the khaki cargo pants, the white baseball caps, and the fleece jackets surrounding me, I decided to fully delve into vampire mode, asserting my individuality by dressing goth and going to goth clubs where I looked exactly like everyone else. I became a regular at a club in Cambridge and there I met Thane, a celibate, weary-eyed vampire who made custom fangs that could easily pop on and off. I had two sets made. A short set for day and a long set for night. For some reason I thought of them like makeup, where appropriateness calls for less during the day and more at night. After a few years of use, the acrylic fangs, once perfectly color-matched to my teeth, yellowed a bit, and by the time I was serious about Jeff it dawned on me how preposterous it was for a twenty-four-year-old to still be running around in fangs. So I retired both sets.

Then, unable to pinpoint my unhappiness in the last year of my marriage, I inexplicably Googled Thane and found him, still in Boston. As luck would have it, his fang business was booming and he was coming to Los Angeles for work in a couple of months. I set up an appointment.

If I thought being twenty-four was too old to be gallivanting around in fangs, twenty-nine was certainly past my vampire prime. But I pulled out an old corset, some black boots, and a Victorianesque skirt. I covered my already alabaster skin in corpse white base and surrounded my eyes with black liner and red shadow. I drove to Thane's friend's apartment, where he was making the fangs. I felt I looked worthy of his velvet cape's embrace. As I knocked on the door with my giant silver rings clanging, I felt like I had been away from my people for too long.

Thane answered the door eyelinerless, wearing a T-shirt and jeans. Jeans are a big goth no-no, like white after Labor Day, men in tank tops, or anything in chartreuse. Thane saw my pale face go even paler and he explained that now in his late thirties making fangs was his business, but being goth was no longer his style. Feeling it was more embarrassing to admit that I had gotten all dressed up like this just to see him, I maintained that I had never given up the goth look.

I ordered an extra-long set of fangs and, after taking a mold of my teeth, Thane completed them within the hour. I drove home wearing them, grinning at people at red lights. As I walked into the condo, touching the sharp tips with my tongue, I felt young again. Maybe even a little immortal. I playfully crawled over to Jeff sitting in his chair and nibbled on his neck. He was unenthused.

This should have been a giant trouble-in-paradise red flag. Along with other items or experiences from your past that you could resurrect, like collecting unicorn figurines, doing triathlons, or going to church, throwing yourself back into something you have left behind often means you are unsettled or unfulfilled with your current life and looking for some sort of comfort in the familiar. I was reverting back to something that, although I logically knew was pure silliness, made me feel in control again.

Buying new fangs was not the only way I reverted to past behaviors during the last year of my marriage, but it was the less dangerous of the two. A month into my MTV job, I decided to buy some cocaine. I felt entitled to have fun, entitled to do my drug of choice since my husband did his all day long, and entitled to rebel (against whom exactly I'm not sure). And since I hadn't touched the stuff in sixteen years, I reasoned it was time to see if I was really addicted or not.

The first time I ever did coke was in a Denny's parking lot on South Beach. I was thirteen years old and it was the summer between eighth and ninth grades. You see, after sixth grade I couldn't bear to follow all the French-braided girls back to private school, so I went back to public school with Jennifer for junior high. The first day of seventh grade I wore a pink miniskirt, black T-shirt, pink E. G. socks, and stark white Keds. No uniform, no snobby private school kids, and the best part: no one there would be calling me Sausage. I walked into school with Jennifer by my side, but we were quickly separated by throngs of students and different homerooms. I trudged through the insanely crowded hallways and amid the boom boxes blaring rap, kids yelling in Spanglish, and general chaos of fights breaking out, I heard, "Snob!" Then I heard it again. I looked around, expecting to see someone from my old school, maybe Christy or Kristen or Crissy, cowering in the corner. But as I continued down the packed hall I realized who the kids were calling a snob. Me.

I was the only white girl in sight and when I focused in on my surroundings, I once again felt like an outsider. Wherever you go, there you are. Instead of dealing with mean rich kids who picked on me because they thought I was weird, I was dealing with kids who had homemade tattoos, understood police codes, and knew how to use a crowbar and they picked on me because they assumed I was a mean rich kid.

Berns had left for college right before I went into seventh grade and Chauncey had moved out long before. Susan had mentally checked out when her mother died the previous year, and spent her days watching soap operas. John, always teetering on an angry and illogical outburst because there were too many giant ketchup bottles from Costco in the cupboard, had a complete nervous breakdown on an airplane. For the next year he wandered around the house taking Xanax and trying to pull himself back together. It felt like the only person I had left was Jennifer.

In seventh grade, I became like a jealous boyfriend, holding on to her tightly because she was the only person who hadn't seemingly abandoned me. I expected her to sit with me at lunch every day and to spend both Friday and Saturday nights with me, eating pizza bagels, going to the movies, and sleeping over. Then, as will happen with twelve-year-old girls, we got into a huge fight in the beginning of eighth grade and we broke up. Then I had no one.

I devised a plan to reinvent myself and befriend a new crowd. The kind of crowd that has tag signs, relatives in jail, and gang affiliations. One day in the spill-out area, the horrible patch of dirt the students were herded into after lunch, I started talking to Maria, a Dominican girl twice my size who seemed to have been around all sorts of blocks. She was amused that the little white girl had the nerve to approach her, and she took me in. I became friends with her and her group and soon had a tag of my own: VAMPIRE. I practiced writing it over and over again in one motion. They would spray-paint their tags on walls. I stuck to doodling my tag on my extremely organized notebooks. And because I started hanging out with Maria, I was no longer called "snob" when I walked through the halls. I bought a gold cross and Z. Cavariccis and started saying "oye" a lot. Susan was amused by the gold cross; John didn't seem to notice.

Maria invited me to her birthday party and there I met her older brother and his guy friends. They were keeping their distance from the junior high kids and sat on a car outside. I, feeling it was time for level two of reinvention, sauntered up to the car, introduced myself, drank beer with them, and then and there became a delinquent. Sure, I had already gotten kicked out of summer camp for drinking an Original Bartles & Jaymes wine cooler, I had already smoked pot with Berns and had a few drinks at family parties, and I had already gone to third base with a boy, at the camp I had been kicked out of. But I knew hanging out with these guys would lead to a whole new league of bad behavior.

I started skipping school to smoke pot, drink beer, and make out with Maria's brother (did I mention he was a drug dealer?) on one of the many golf courses in Miami Beach. At any moment we could have been arrested for trespassing, underage drinking, or illegal drug use, but it didn't even dawn on me to worry about this possibility. And like John never checking the car mileage during my first year with Billy, the police never checked behind the giant billowing golf course trees so they never caught me and Maria's brother.

I didn't even like the taste of beer or the way pot made me feel, but I relished feeling like an adult. To me swapping spit with a seventeen-year-old drug dealer, skipping school, drinking beer, and smoking marijuana was all very adult. And for such an older guy to like me, I must be really, really mature. I mean, why else would he be spending so much time with me?

The brother and I hung out for a few weeks and then things petered out. I was waiting for him to pick me up at a friend's house when he stood me up. I remember being hurt but instead of admitting that to myself, I focused on what a waste of newly shaved legs it was. All the brother and I had done was kiss, and although he was a drug dealer, we only did pot. So on the scale of bad-news guys, he wasn't anywhere near the heaviest. His friend Diego was really heavy. He was nineteen and had a mustache and he was the one who first gave me coke. A month later I gave him my virginity. If a seventeen-year-old liking me made me feel grown-up, a nineteen-year-old giving me attention made me feel even more adult and capable of being autonomous. I didn't need Susan and John to pay attention to me anyway. I didn't need Jennifer to have lunch with me or Berns to still be living in the house giving me rock quizzes on the Who and the Doors. And I didn't need Chauncey to take an interest in my daily life from his faraway home in Seattle. I didn't need anyone and would live my life just the way I wanted. Which happened to be with an unemployed, mustached, drug-using, statutory-raping high school dropout and gang member.

I describe that first time I did coke best in my diary.

I tried cocaine! It's the coolest fucking thing on Earth! I think I'm addicted. Oh well.

It *was* the coolest fucking thing on Earth. Looking back it kind of felt like getting dragged under a train and surviving. When I was wired, I was strong, smart, powerful, and fast. And because I was so young and had no life experience, I didn't take any of it all that seriously. Addiction? Whatever. Getting shot at while copping drugs in the ghetto? Exciting! Overdosing? That only happens to people who don't know what they're doing.

Those next three months with Diego were manic fun. Growing up in Miami, it just seemed to me that doing cocaine was a required part of adolescence, like getting a bat mitzvah or a driver's license. And now that I was surrounded by other teens doing a ton of coke, it didn't even seem that bad. Susan could tell I wasn't "centered" and she didn't approve, but she didn't do much in the way of discipline. I think she was at a loss. John, always in his office, writing his latest book, didn't notice I was on the precipice of being the star and object lesson of an After-School Special.

Then ninth grade started and, being the consummate good student always looking toward Yale (because even at my most rebellious I still wanted to make John proud by going to his alma mater), I never let my grades drop. Sure, I might have come to class wired a couple of times, but I still studied and cared about my GPA. Jennifer and I started talking again and a girl I had been partying with started to spend time with a much older guy who would give her coke. I'm not talking nineteen older, I'm talking sixty older. For me, this was the clear line between teenage rebellion and do-anything-for-drugs addiction.

So with the help of a school counselor I decided my delinquency phase, which lasted a year from start to finish, needed to end. I went home and told Susan and John I might be a drug addict and I started going to Narcotics Anonymous meetings. Now, I'm not sure, to this day, that I was in fact a drug addict. I think I was certainly acting out, desperate for my parents to give me attention in the form of discipline. I definitely used coke to feel powerful when I felt most powerless and thought being liked by older guys meant I was pretty and worthy and not a sausage. But when all this failed to make me feel better in the long term, as in for more than twenty minutes at a time, and when Susan and John still didn't give me any parameters, amazingly I had enough self-preservation to decide to stop the bad behavior all on my own. I stopped before I was arrested, murdered, pregnant, or raped. I stopped before the cocaine use became a physical addiction, instead of just an emotional crutch.

In NA, you learn you are powerless against your drug. You learn one is too many, a thousand never enough, and that once an addict, always an addict. They teach you that if you do consume anything of a drink or drug nature, you will be led back to your drug of choice. I ate up all this rhetoric and enjoyed being sanctimonious and spouting slogans at Susan and John as they drank their glass of wine with dinner. I put a bumper sticker on the mirror in my bathroom that read, "Drugs: They Just Aren't Cool Anymore." I loved that sticker because it acknowledged that drugs were at some point cool and just because they cease to be cool doesn't mean you have to pretend they were never awesome to begin with.

After I stopped doing drugs, retired my gold cross and chain, and ended my delinquent phase, I lavished in my new phase of being in recovery. The daily meetings and clear-cut steps made me feel like a part of something and gave me specific rules, boundaries, guidelines, and what I craved most, order. And I got to know some really great transgender recovering crack addicts. Something not every fourteen-year-old can say.

At Boston College I chose to live in the substance-free dorms, where if anyone was caught with alcohol or drugs they would be immediately expelled. In other dorms, they would get a slap on the wrist. I liked being surrounded by uptight, sober people instead of puke. And although I had not been to an NA meeting since I was fifteen, I didn't touch alcohol again until I was twenty years old. It was at my cousin's wedding that I felt I was done with the straight-edge phase. I felt like I could have a glass of wine, so I did. Then I waited to see what would happen. I didn't explode or implode and I didn't run back to cocaine. I wondered if I had ever really been addicted in the first place.

Then, at twenty-nine years old, feeling dismissed by my husband who never wanted to spend time with me and feeling all grown up because I had a cool writing job on a cool TV show, I asked an assistant I could tell would know because of his fauxhawk and skinny jeans where I might score some blow. He did know, and the next day he had a gram for me. Then I told Jeff I had bought some coke because I thought it might be fun to do every now and again. Jeff knew all about my past and I think some part of me wanted him to say, "Let's figure out why you feel you want that in your life again." Or, "What the fuck are you thinking?" Or, "No way am I letting you start that." Maybe I wanted him to react the way Susan and

John never reacted. I wanted to heal those old wounds by replaying it and ending with a different outcome. But because Jeff either didn't care, didn't see that it was a huge warning sign, or felt it would be too hypocritical to tell me not to do drugs when he himself did them, he just said, "Okay."

His apathetic reaction just gave me more license to do it and made me feel that perhaps I had been overreacting about being addicted all those years ago. My own parents weren't that concerned when I was thirteen and now my husband wasn't that concerned. So why should I be concerned?

And because I wondered for so long if I was really addicted to coke, I thought the only way to truly find out was to do it again. If I could do it again, and stop when I wanted to, then clearly I wasn't addicted. Foolproof logic, I know. So I set forth some rules. I would only do it at most once a week. If I could leave it untouched sitting in a drawer for days at a time then that for sure was verification I wasn't addicted. Because clearly I couldn't keep my hands off mint chip ice cream for more than ten minutes.

So my weekly ritual began. Sundays when Jeff would leave for his bartending job, I would set out the cocaine on a colored piece of construction paper. The bright pink and purple made me happiest. I would put a little pile of coke in the middle of the paper, admiring the stark whiteness against the bright colors, and cut it up with my LA Fitness card. I always enjoyed the irony in that. And I would do a couple of lines, then I would do the laundry and watch *Footballers' Wives*, a delectable British soap opera. Sometimes I would clean. Sometimes I would pace. When the last load of laundry was in the dryer, I would put the cute little packet of powder back in a little jewelry box in my dresser. I would throw away the neon piece of paper with the slightest trace of white marks left on it and I would feel good about my weekly ritual.

After a few months of this I was convinced I was in fact not addicted. Not now and not before. It took me months to get through a gram. I was able to put it back each Sunday and not think about it again until the following Sunday. I was entitled to a little fun, so I bought another gram. I started doing a few lines secretly here and there just to see if Jeff would notice if I was acting differently. He never did. No one seemed to notice, which proved to me that I didn't have a drug problem. Then Jeff and I split up, and I started doing a few lines before I would go out with my friends. You know, just to make getting ready more fun. I would put on loud music, dance around the condo, and try on outfits. When I arrived wherever I was going, I would immediately have a drink to cool off. I bought an eight-ball, which is three and a half grams, and then I started bringing my little glass vile with me and doing a few bumps while I was out, to stay energized, awake, and unhungry. Then I started getting nosebleeds.

Had I learned nothing since I was thirteen? Drugs: They *Still* Just Aren't Cool Anymore.

At dinner one night, as I moved my salad around my plate barely eating, my friend Aaron said he was concerned because I seemed manic. No one else commented, assuming I was just under divorce stress. When I went to get my hair done a couple of months later, my hairdresser, whom I had been with for four years, took one look at me and said, "Girl, you look busted." He sat me in front of the mirror and pointed out my red nose, my dry skin, and my bloodshot eyes. He made me drink three bottles of water while I sat in his chair, and he told me: "Stop it!" Once I could see that my weekly nonaddiction was leading to an addiction and I no longer even had Jeff around to not notice I put an end to the cocaine use, again. I unceremoniously flushed the remains down the drain and was grateful to discover that watching *Footballers' Wives* drug free was just as riveting.

Step 22

Go from Bubbles to Sawdust on Valentine's Day

For all her avoiding of sentimental drivel, Susan always had fun with Valentine's Day. I would wake up on February fourteenth and see a shiny wrapped present at the foot of my bed. It could be earrings, fun socks, or a stuffed animal, and always a glitter-encrusted card smothered with hearts. I intellectually understand that the holiday is just a marketing ploy. A reason to schlep to the Hallmark store and buy crap, to eat overpriced chocolate and buy marked-up roses, and for men to have to do nice things for the woman they are trying to sleep with or want to continue sleeping with. But Valentine's Day is also a reason to tell someone they have a secret admirer, to show love and affection, and for stoic mothers to give their daughters glittery cards with hearts. And that is never a bad thing.

On our first Valentine's Day, Jeff and I agreed we didn't need to battle the crowds at a restaurant or exchange gifts or do anything expensive. Yet he shocked me with his simple yet romantic gestures that evening. He brought me into my bathroom, glimmering with candlelight, and I saw my bathtub filled with bubbles. He instructed me to relax for twenty minutes while he cooked us dinner. I soaked in the luxurious water and when I got out Jeff did the most amazing thing. He wrapped me in a towel right out of the dryer. It was warm and soft and that small detail was so incredibly thoughtful, I was floored. It really was a Valentine's Day filled with love.

On our last Valentine's Day together, I had been working at MTV for a few months. The joke at the office was, "Is Sascha really married, or is she just making it up?" because no one had met Jeff. He didn't go to any parties or come out for after-work drinks or stop by for lunch, like the other significant others often did. I wanted my coworkers to meet Jeff and see that I did in fact have a husband, and he was charming and adorable, and I wanted that producer who had jokingly asked me if I was happy at home to see that I was happy at home. I wanted the assistant who was selling me grams to know that just because I did the occasional blow didn't mean I wasn't in a good marriage. So I asked Jeff, as a special Valentine's present to me, could he please come pick me up at MTV for lunch, meet some of my coworkers, and bring me pretty flowers so I could have them on my desk to remind me of his affection.

By most people's standards, to meet some of your wife's coworkers, bring her flowers, and have lunch with her is not a high-maintenance request. But since on the four Valentine's Days prior to this one I had made no requests, this seemed extremely demanding to Jeff. But he begrudgingly agreed. He finally showed up at MTV an hour late. He was drenched in sweat and complaining about the traffic and the long drive over the hill. He thrust a dozen beautiful pink roses into my hands while bitching about how expensive they were and how long he had to stand in line to purchase them. He mustered a smile and met some of my office friends. Then we went to lunch. Because Jeff had arrived so late, the place I had picked out was now closed. He was in no mood to drive to yet another location, so he pointed to a restaurant across the street and said, "Let's just eat there."

I already felt guilty about asking him to drive all the way to see me at work and to buy the flowers, clearly a difficult purchase, so I didn't want to be any more demanding. And even though I had a bad feeling about the restaurant across the street I agreed. The place had a dingy orange awning with tan lettering. It had a beer-battered corn dog feel and the floor was covered in sawdust. I could tell they were going for down-home, earthy décor and using the sawdust as a lazy ploy to never have to mop the floor. It was filthy.

But I plopped down at the table and cheerfully looked over the sticky menu. I ordered a coffee, and a few minutes after it arrived I accidentally knocked it over. Coffee spilled across the table and dripped onto the sawdusted floor. This is when the Valentine's Day went from depressing to atrocious. Jeff flew off the handle and started yelling at me.

"What is wrong with you? I have to clean up spilled drinks all night at the bar and now I'm here and I have to clean up spilled drinks for you!"

I should have walked out, walked back to MTV, and called a divorce lawyer then and there. But instead, crushed and confused, I tried to reason with him.

"You don't have to clean it up. The waitress will. We can leave a bigger tip. I'll leave the tip. I'm sorry, I didn't mean to spill the coffee."

As he drove me back to MTV I had the distinct feeling he didn't like me anymore. Maybe on some level he loved me, but it was clear he didn't like me. How could he, and be so cruel? He hated that I wanted to tell him about my intricately detailed dreams every morning. He despised that I would excitedly call him on my way home from work, instead of just waiting to talk to him in person. He dismissed it when I got a Brazilian wax and took pole-dancing classes to try to add some color back into our usual paint-by-numbers pallet. Doing nice things for me once brought him joy, and now it just magnified his resentment.

On paper, and on Valentine's Day, he did everything I asked. He came to MTV, brought me flowers, and took me to lunch. But he also made sure to let me know he was annoyed to the point of furious about the entire request.

He didn't think I was worth the half hour drive, getting stuck in traffic, waiting in line at a flower shop, or meeting my coworkers. And he certainly didn't think I was worth being treated with respect when I accidentally spilled a drink. I don't know if he loved me then or not, but he certainly didn't like me and after that day, I certainly did not like him.

Step 23

When a Handsome Stranger Gives You His Card, Keep It

My grandmother on Susan's side always used to say, "It's just as easy to fall in love with a rich man as it is with a poor man." For me this wasn't true. I was always drawn to the starving artists, the dreamers, the guys with possibilities instead of trust funds. But when Berns and I were having one of our many sisters' weekends in Vegas, I met a rich guy. And he didn't seem all that bad. Berns and I were sitting at a restaurant at the Bellagio when a napkin caught on fire. Berns rushed to put it out and got the attention of two gentlemen at the bar.

Although I was married, and Berns was in a serious relationship, it was immediately clear who was "my" guy and who was "her" guy. My guy was tall, dark, and handsome and looked like a Boston lawyer, in conservative pleated slacks, loafers, and a dark jacket. He was in his early forties and single and in fact *was* a Boston lawyer. The four of us had many drinks at the bar and then walked over to a blackjack table. Berns and "her" guy, a friendly, shorter blond, chatted away about all sorts of things, including his wife and kids and Berns's boyfriend. It was clear there was zero sexual tension between them, and it was just going to be a friendly Vegas encounter.

My guy, however, made my stomach flip when he placed his hand on the small of my back as we walked toward an open table. As well as buying all our drinks, he gave me money to gamble with, and he helped me decide when to hit and when to stay. We played for hours and whenever my stack would get low, more chips would appear. He was fascinated by my long red hair, my black nails, my mermaid tattoo, and the ups and downs of my Los Angeles writing career. He thought of me as an exotic, daring, wild creature, usually not found among Boston professionals.

I was fascinated that he wore a suit to work every day. He not only had health insurance but provided it for *his* employees at *his* firm. He was responsible and adultlike. He didn't play video games or smoke pot or even own a hoodie. He had a briefcase, not a backpack or messenger bag, and he had plenty of money. He wasn't a nouveau riche, Porsche-driving tool but a sensible, Volvo-driving man, who happened to be wealthy.

After a long and intoxicatingly fun night of drinking, eating, and gambling, we made a plan to meet up with the guys the following night. Berns and I went back to our hotel and I kept her up until dawn, asking her why I felt so stuck, unsettled, and unsatisfied. Why did I dread going back home to Jeff?

The next night my guy took us all out to dinner, where we each shared incredibly personal stories. The kind of stories you tell on airplanes when you assume you will never see your seatmate again. Then we gambled the night away, me with a never-ending stack of chips. When it was time once again to return to our respective hotels, my guy gave me his card. He said, "I know you're married. But if you're ever not married, please do call me. I think you are phenomenal."

I hugged him good-bye and put the card away in a safe place.

Step 24

Have Friends Who Are Also Getting Divorced by Thirty

Once I realized I didn't want Jeff at my birthday party I started to confide to my closest friends about my unhappiness. Maybe divorce is catching. Once a friend does it, you realize it's a viable option, like getting a tattoo or committing suicide. Or maybe divorce isn't contagious and it's just a coincidence that at twenty-nine years old, most of my friends were also unhappy in their marriages.

It's easy to sum up someone else's relationship, because from the outside the mistakes and missteps look so obvious.

Marry a Comedian

Michelle shocked me when she told me she too was miserable. I thought she had a great relationship, filled with laughter, teamwork, and adoration, but when she peeled back the layers I could see her pain. Her husband was a successful stand-up comic and what I learned from her is that marrying a comedian is even worse than marrying an actor. Comedians are not only battling between total self-absorption and insecurity, they are also constantly trying to be funny.

Move In Together to Save Money

I was not shocked to hear my friend Aaron was getting divorced, because it was clear he had been suffering for years. After getting married, Aaron was a shell of his once charmingly acerbic self. He was like a beleaguered sitcom husband, except instead of "take my wife, please" jokes, there was just animosity.

His path to getting divorced by thirty was to move in with his girlfriend way too quickly, using the excuse that it made financial sense. They lived in New York City at the time. Once they had moved in together, they fell into wedding plans and a marriage. Their wedding was spectacular: guys in gorilla costumes and everything. But once again, the wedding does not make the marriage. I happened to work with his wife briefly, and after a big fight with him she received four dozen roses at the office. She was pacified but I knew his apology was meaningless because all it took was for him to make a phone call and give his credit card number and, bam, he was done. It was a quick and impermanent fix instead of sitting down with her and really talking about their insurmountable problems.

Like many men, Aaron did not leave his wife even though he admitted to being unhappy. He just brooded in quiet misery until she left him. And good for her that she did.

All Your Friends Are Doing It

Like a Christian kid doing the bar mitzvah circuit in eighth grade, you can feel pretty left out if you're not part of the twenty-seven-year-olds' wedding circuit. No parties. No presents. No center of attention. That's how my friend Liz felt, so she decided it was time to get a boyfriend quick, and get married even quicker. She married the first person that came along. Even though he was in an awful band, called her the wrong name in bed once, and never paid for dinner. Liz's marriage lasted only three months.

Ignore Your Spouse and Dive into a New Addiction

To escape from his daily discontentment my friend Robert started playing World of Warcraft constantly. One night he called me and asked if it was a bad sign that his wife had started getting Brazilian waxes when they hadn't had sex in months. He just happened to see it when she was getting out of the shower. I told him she was cheating. Once Robert hit level 70 of the game, his wife admitted to having an affair with a coworker and left him.

Beat a Dead Horse

This general, late-twenties relationship melancholy transcends sexual orientation. Although not technically married, my friend Alise went to the West Hollywood courthouse to get domestic-partner papers with her live-in girlfriend of three years. A year later, Alise was tired of the lesbian bed death, the constant talking riddled with miscommunications, and the biweekly therapy sessions. Marriage can be hard but it shouldn't be that hard, and if it is, it's time to leave. The brink of thirty is a good age to realize that beating a dead horse won't make it move any faster.

During the mass marriage exodus, a few of my friends maintained strong, healthy relationships. Jennifer and her husband were holding steady and the Altadena lawyers were happy. And Owen, my old friend who officiated at my wedding, got engaged while the rest of us were getting divorced. Just in case divorce was catching, he asked us all to stay far, far away from him and his lovely fiancée. But I assured him he was safe since he was already thirty.

Aaron, Alise, Liz, Robert, Michelle, and I all got divorced

within a month of each other. Although not planned, Michelle and I actually left our husbands on the same day. Each couple had varying degrees of fighting, sadness, and aftermath. But because no one had children, what to do with our condos seemed to be the biggest hurdle.

Like Aaron and Robert, Jeff waited for me to decide to leave. It seems men are more comfortable with status quo, even if that status sucks. Even Alise, who was sort of the "girl" in her relationship, made the decision to leave her wife. After extensive research, my expert theory is that most men are ultimately too lazy to get divorced. The numbing misery is better than the paperwork.

Step 25

Tell People at a Party You Are Getting Divorced, Before You Tell Your Husband

I was on my way to an unofficial *Late Late Show with Craig Kilborn* reunion party. I wasn't sure if the Devil was going to be there and I hadn't seen him for several years. I knew he had gotten married and then divorced. I also knew that he knew I had gotten married. When I walked into the crowded bar area, I saw Owen immediately and started chatting with people.

"You look so great!"

"Thanks, so do you!"

"What have you been up to?"

"Oh, you know, writing. The usual."

"Want some hummus?"

"Yes!"

And then I saw a wisp of shaggy hair hanging over a

dangerous smile. It was the Devil, and he was staring at me. We chatted about the past several years. He made a joke about his divorce and then he asked me how my marriage was going. Without a beat I said, "Oh, I'm getting a divorce." He said he was sorry to hear that and reminded me that he had a house in the Cape for the summer and I was welcome to stop by anytime.

It was then that I knew I had to go home and tell Jeff.

Step 26

Don't Fight to Save the Marriage

I drove home, heart pounding. I had said the words and now it was time to say them to my husband. I got home and Jeff wasn't there. I paced around the condo: the one I had wanted so badly to own. When he finally got home I was lying on the bed. He walked into the bedroom and I sat up and said, "I need to talk to you."

There was a chair in the bedroom. A sturdy antique wooden chair upholstered in orange and red. Although it was comfortable, no one ever sat in it, not even Spork. It just sort of stayed in the corner adding color to the room. Jeff, seeing the grave look on my face, sat down in that chair. I remember thinking it was strange that for such a momentous conversation he was sitting in a chair we so rarely used. It was as if we had placed it there two years earlier knowing one day this conversation would come.

"I'm unhappy. I think we should get a divorce."

He looked at me, not shocked, sort of numb, probably

stoned, and said, "Okay." I like to think he said this next, but it came a day or two later: "My pot and my chair were here before you. My pot and my chair will be here after you." That was his way of saying I had been an inconsequential blip in the epic adventure of his life, in which his constant companions needed only to be his pot and his chair. He was not going to fight to keep me. Of course he had been unhappy too, and once he got over the initial hurt of me saying it first, he quickly realized it was what he wanted also. Although he told me to take a week and think about it, we both knew the decision was already made. We didn't discuss going to couples therapy or trying to solve our problems or even trying to determine what they really were. We had both given up long before.

Several months before this moment, in a moment of hopeful communication, I came home from work and told Jeff I was unhappy. He said, "Yeah, let's give it a couple weeks. If you're still unhappy, we'll get a divorce." We laughed, once again downplaying our marriage and what it meant to us. I asked him then if he wanted to move back to the beach. We could sell the condo. It wasn't worth his happiness and our happiness together. He said no, we should keep it. It was a good investment. Then I asked him if he would ever consider stopping smoking pot. He said no. I couldn't blame him since I married him knowing full well what his habits were. He told me in no uncertain terms on my twenty-fourth birthday, five and a half years before, that he would not stop smoking pot. So he was unwilling to make any changes and he wasn't asking me to make any changes. So that was that.

I felt terribly guilty and blamed myself for everything. I took this nice Chicago guy, who was minding his own business, and forced him to buy new glasses, forced him into marriage, forced him to the Valley, then left him. I see now I blamed myself and discounted Jeff's free will because it was easier for me to feel like the bad guy, the guy in control, than to feel deeply hurt by his neglect.

That night I slept on the daybed in the office, wrapped in a velvet blanket with tassels Berns had made me years before. Jeff got the bedroom because the daybed was too small for him. Spork didn't seem too concerned by the change in sleeping arrangements and managed to wedge himself next to me on the narrow daybed.

Jeff and I never kissed again. It was weird to think the last time we had kissed, we were both unaware it was going to be the last time. After the divorce discussion we barely had any physical contact at all. We continued to live together for another couple of weeks, passing each other awkwardly in the hall, being overly courteous and friendly. But when we would both end up in the living room, watching Ruby, it was like nothing had changed. We were in our comfort zone sitting there together, now disconnected.

There was no yelling, anger, or hostility. Not on the surface anyway. We reviewed where it all went wrong. Jeff jokingly blamed MTV for our divorce since I had been working there for the past year. I jokingly blamed the Cubs since they of course didn't play well that year. We said we always knew it wouldn't last forever, but we had made a good go of it. One night Jeff came into my room, perched himself on the edge of the daybed, and apologized. He said, "I don't want you to blame yourself. I have not been a good husband." I was so relieved to hear him admit that but also unprepared to face the emotional implications.

Jeff and I didn't need a lawyer since we weren't contesting anything. We would sell the condo and split the profits, if there were any. We each took a bookshelf, books already divided, and split up some of the wedding presents. Jeff would take Ruby and pay me for half of her. I, of course, would keep Spork. The plan was for Jeff to move out once he found an apartment in Venice and I would stay in the condo until it sold. When our friends called to see how we were doing, we told everyone it was the best divorce ever. And in many ways, it was. No fighting. No horrible drag-out battles over stuff. No trying to get revenge on each other. We both really just wanted out.

Step 27

Believe in the "Get the First One Over With" Philosophy

A week after the divorce conversation, I flew to Miami to get away, give Jeff some space, and tell my parents I was getting divorced. I wasn't sure exactly how I was going to say it, or how they would react. Would John be mad about giving us a down payment? Would Susan want back her gold necklace that she gave me at my shower? Would they be disappointed in me?

As I walked out of the airport into a thick wall of humidity I felt at home again, comforted by the familiar sights, sounds, and smells and immediate sweat. Susan and John picked me up outside of arrivals (no one in my family ever parked and went in), and I hopped in the back of the car. I was going to wait until we got home to tell them the news but minutes after being picked up, while driving over the causeway, I blurted out that Jeff and I were done. That's when Susan sighed and said, "It's very sad when a five-year marriage only lasts two and a half years." Then John asked if I had a quarter for the toll.

I was furious and thought to myself, *I am getting a divorce! Didn't you hear me? And all you care about is a quarter for the toll!* But then I realized that life goes on. John needs a quarter. Just because I'm getting a divorce doesn't mean the toll doesn't need to be paid. So I gave him a quarter. Susan said she was not surprised by this news in the least and that she knew I had been unhappy for a while. I sat in the back of the car, stunned at their casualness. Then their unruffled attitude washed over me and calmed me down considerably. Susan noticing I was unhappy helped justify my decision. Like when you have a gnawing pain and you finally go to the doctor and he says, "Well, it's a good thing you came in. You have a torn tendon." You feel relieved that there is an actual problem and a solution and you aren't crazy. Susan supplied my second opinion and relieved me of any possible second-guessing. Yes, I had been unhappy, and now I was taking needed actions to make myself happy. And it was just divorce, after all. Scary, but I would get through it and come out the other end new and improved.

Susan and John, who have been together for over thirty-five years, both believe in getting the first one over with. Susan's first husband was a charming, philandering cad who gambled all their wedding money away on their honeymoon. And although his death left her a widow, they were already heading toward divorce. John had so little to say to his first wife he avoided being alone with her on their honeymoon, taking a rowboat to a small diner to escape the isolation of their romantic cabin getaway.

My parents both seemed to learn from the mistakes they made the first time around and because their second try was such a success, they are big believers in the "get divorced by thirty" philosophy. I grew up hearing snippets about each of their first spouses, and understood that sometimes you have to make the wrong choice to get to the right one. And although Susan sometimes annoys John to no end by constantly asking, "Where are my glasses?" and John upsets Susan when he steals her stories and pretends they happened to him, and neither of them says "I love you" to the other one, the two of them are clearly in love. Year after year they laugh and support each other and make bets on everything from the capital of Bangladesh to who starred in *Hee Haw*, bets that Susan always wins. They have adventures together, they stick out the bad times, and when they fight they always make up. So I grew up seeing that marriage can work and does work. Just maybe not the first marriage.

Having gotten my first one over with, I felt a certain pride that week in Miami. A closeness with my parents now that I was experiencing a rite of passage that they had both gone through. Susan and John certainly had some major chinks in their parenting armor, but this was one time when they were fully there for me. They listened and understood without escalating the situation. No hysterics, no drama, and no need for major changes in my life plan. I didn't need to buy a villa in Tuscany or find an ashram in India to get through my divorce.

Susan, the consummate book giver, was sad to see Jeff go because she had finally gotten a handle on what he liked to read. John, who had been a nerd for the first fifty years of his life and then turned into a mountain-climbing, cycling überjock, was going to miss watching couch potatoes Jeff and Ray play video games with the zeal of Tour de France riders. And we were all going to feel the loss of no longer being related to the Nicest Woman in the World. Losing her as a mother-in-law was a painful but unavoidable part of the process.

That week when Jeff told his family I wanted a divorce, they were convinced we would work it out and I was just trying to avoid rewriting my latest script. They thought that I imagined a divorce would be the perfect thing to distract me from the hideous task in front of me. I thought this take was extremely funny, and probably not that unviable, but it wasn't true. At this point I was much too aware of my feelings to be tricked by procrastination. Just to prove them wrong, I finished my rewrites before we even divided up the Pottery Barn plates.

Step 28

Take Out the Garbage

A few uncomfortable days after I returned from Miami, Jeff signed a lease and Ray came over to help him move out. I didn't mean to be home for the move but timed it a bit wrong and walked in just as Jeff was walking out for the last time. Ray glared at me without saying a word. Jeff gave me a knowing nod and said, "Well, 'bye." And I said, "Good-bye," and Jeff was gone.

Although it would take six months for us to be legally divorced, once his La-Z-Boy was gone it felt immediate. I stood where it once sat and was filled with dread and joy. Spork came out of the bedroom to sniff around all the extra space.

I slowly walked through the now half-empty condo in a daze, feeling as if I were in purgatory. Everything was in flux. It wasn't my home anymore, but I didn't have a new one. I would be legally divorced soon but technically wasn't yet. I was on the precipice of a seemingly momentous birthday but wasn't quite there. This overwhelming feeling of transition was paralyzing, and I just stood in the center of the living room and stared at the blank walls where Jeff's artwork and pictures had once been. I glanced into the kitchen and saw the garbage.

Jeff had been taking out the garbage for years. It was my least favorite job, and one he naturally adopted once we moved in together. Maybe I'm doing a disservice to women's lib but I always thought that taking out the garbage was dirty, smelly, unwieldy, and, in my opinion, a man's job. All of a sudden it hit me: I was going to have to take out the garbage myself.

Before I understood what was happening, the tears welled up in my eyes, and I crumpled to the floor and sobbed. This was the second time I really cried during my entire divorce process. It wasn't about the trash. It was about the death of my relationship, but it was much easier to concentrate on the garbage. So after a few minutes of self-indulgent keening, I picked myself off the floor, marched over to the garbage, pulled the bag out of the can, and bravely took it to the Dumpster down the hall.

After tossing it into the stinky Dumpster, I felt a surge of accomplishment. I thought, if the worst part of divorce was taking the garbage out, I was going to be just fine.

The other thing Jeff had always provided was quarters for the laundry. I never let change accumulate, because I never let anything accumulate. So finding quarters for laundry was always an unpleasant challenge for me. Because Jeff was a bartender, he had endless change from tips, which he would throw into a giant plastic Heineken bottle piggy bank. Once it was full he would take it to a Coinstar and buy himself a treat. But as it filled up, I was allowed to dip in for laundry. I now realized that Jeff's Heineken bottle was gone with him.

I began to cry again. *I don't have any quarters. How will I do the laundry? How am I going to handle all this on my own? What have I done? I'm all alone.* I let the panic pass and then thought logically about where one might get quarters. I decided a bank would be my best bet. I breathed deeply, blew my nose, and splashed cold water on my face. I drove myself to the Washington Mutual and I got myself a roll of quarters. It was invigorating.

That week I also bought myself a new TV, two inches bigger than Ruby, and named it Stringer Bell, a character from my favorite show, *The Wire*. But once Jeff was out of my life, I rarely watched Stringer because I had so many other things to keep me busy. I frantically cleaned the condo so it was spotless for the hordes of people that came to the open houses. I went to the gym. I wrote and rewrote. I spent time with all my friends who were also in the midst of a divorce. And, on a trip back from the Dumpster one day, I ran into the sexy, dirty guy who lived upstairs. He asked, "Where's your man?" I told him he had left, that we had gotten a divorce. And this thirty-five-year-old who still lived with his parents and rode a bicycle around the neighborhood because his license was suspended for never paying off tickets said, "He was a loser. Not good enough for you anyway."

One night a few days after Jeff moved out, I met Michelle for drinks at a bar off the Pacific Coast Highway. A strange phenomenon occurred as we two newly divorced twenty-nine-year-olds watched the sunset. We both saw each other's eyes for the first time in years. Hers were deep brown glowing with yellow specs. Mine light blue glowing with green rays. Our eyes were alive and bright, like the eyes of werewolves finally being released from their human prisons. We stared at each other in amazement. We were independent, free, and ready to make a whole new set of mistakes in our thirties.

My first mistake was going to be making out with the sexy, dirty guy who lived upstairs.

Step 29

Call Your First Love, Again, and Then Call the Handsome Stranger

I hadn't seen Billy since the end of my senior year of college, so it had been eight years. Although we had kept in touch, especially over the past few months, we did not e-mail pictures to each other. I had called Billy and found out that he and his live-in girlfriend had just broken up. Now that I was getting divorced Billy and I both needed to see each other once again and figure out why we kept coming back. For Billy, I think I had remained a constant in his life all those years because I represented a time when he felt most safe, secure, and loved. So whenever he was in the midst of change, like graduating from college or ending a long relationship, he wanted to come back to me. And before I could really examine myself and my failed marriage and learn from my decisions, I had to give in to my familiar longing for Billy, and see if by any chance being with him would solve all my problems.

Would I even recognize him? Would he be as beautiful as I remembered? Would he still think I was beautiful? My heart pounded and my teeth chattered because I was so nervous. I saw him walking toward me. He was even taller than I remembered and had filled out. His once lean teenage frame had turned into a muscular, toned thirty-year-old man's frame. His broad shoulders and his small waist formed a perfect V and made him look like a super-hero. A bronze superhero with short, spiky black hair. My wavy red hair was a few inches past my boobs, even lon-ger than it was in high school. I knew Billy always loved me with long hair. Divorce stress, and a mild cocaine habit, had helped me to lose more weight, so I was now even skinnier than I was at my wedding. During the flight to meet him I had kept replaying a fantasy of Billy hug-ging my thin body, picking me up, and spinning me around and around, long hair twirling.

We were at the baggage claim in the Las Vegas airport. He had never been to Vegas and I wanted to show him all the things I loved about that town: magicians, showgirls, drinks covered with dry ice smoke, old ladies attached to oxygen tanks playing slots, the glitz of the Strip, the des-titution of Old Town, and the feeling that at any second you could hit it big or fail miserably. A similar vibe I ap-preciated in Los Angeles. I was enamored with the bright lights, the over-the-top décor, the debauchery, the excess, and the mingling of desperation and hope. And I thought it was the perfect place to meet Billy.

He flew there from Tampa, I from Los Angeles. We were spending three nights in a hotel just off the Strip and planned on seeing once again if we were meant to be together. When Billy and I finally stood in front of each other, with our weekend bags, there was no intense embrace or twirling hair. We sort of awkwardly hugged. Then we walked out to get a cab.

Billy, always a believer that his body was his temple, never drank or did drugs. This was one of the reasons he was perfect for me in high school. Although I had already desecrated my temple, it was cleaned and rebuilt by the time I met him, so our temples were straight edge together. Billy also didn't enjoy gambling. Looking back, I'm not sure Vegas was the best place for us to meet.

It was good to see him. And we had a nice time walking down the Strip and seeing shows and shopping. We didn't drink and we didn't gamble. Perhaps because once again the memories were more intense than the reality, time together in the room only got us so far. By eleven p.m. on the first night Billy was exhausted from the jet lag so he went to sleep with his hand on my head. I was wide-awake lying there next to a man I had dreamed about on and off for nearly fifteen years, realizing he was not the answer.

When we returned to the airport three days later, we gave each other a deep hug. We both knew where we stood so there was no longer any awkwardness. We would always keep in touch and be friends. But we were not in love with each other and we both finally recognized it, for good. Sometimes you need to revisit the past to know it's not supposed to be the future.

A month later, after Googling the Handsome Stranger I had met with Berns in Vegas and vetting that he was in fact who he claimed he was, I called him. Eli told me he wanted to have an adventure and he would take me anywhere in the world I wanted to go. I wanted to go to Iceland. His travel agent booked a six-night trip and a month later we were on a flight to Reykjavik. Eli was just as dapper as I had remembered and I was beyond thrilled to be with him and on my way to a country with astounding views, northern lights, beautiful people, fantastic restaurants, and luxury hotels.

We got along extremely well and had a lovely time sightseeing and chatting. There was definitely chemistry between us, but at night, when he was sleeping and loudly snoring and I was wide-awake, I thought about how weird it was to be on the other side of the world and still feel the same exact gnawing uncertainty I felt at home. When I eventually couldn't take the snoring any longer I got out of the plush bed smothered in Egyptian cotton sheets, threw on some clothes, and made my way down to the extravagantly chic hotel lobby. I got to know the waitstaff and sat and drank coffee as they did their end-of-the-night side work and gossiped about the clientele.

By our last day in Iceland, I was certain that I had had

a fantastic trip and I was thrilled that I had met Eli and trusted my instincts enough to travel with him. But I was also certain Eli was not the answer either. No one thing was the answer, not cocaine, not fangs, not ending up with my first love, and not traveling the world with a rich guy. As much as I hate self-help rhetoric, I could no longer ignore that the answer was going to have to come from me.

So a few weeks later when Eli called from Boston and asked me where in the world I wanted to go next, I told him I didn't want to go anywhere. I had too much to sort out at home.

Step 30

Arrive at Your Thirtieth Birthday Party Single

By the time my birthday arrived, Jeff had been gone for four months, I had become a pro at getting quarters and taking out the trash, and I had discovered there wasn't going to be a quick and easy end to my love story. Susan and Berns flew out for my birthday. We had lunch at the Four Seasons, drank Bellinis, and discussed marriage, Berns still not seeing the point and me still not sure, but still inexplicably a believer in the institution. Susan was too buzzed to impart any wisdom. After lunch we went shopping in Beverly Hills and Susan offered to buy me a birthday outfit but nothing seemed to look quite right. I didn't want to buy something just because I could. It occurred to me I could buy something and then return it later and get store credit, but that seemed wrong to do, since the point was that the item be a birthday present. So, with a shockingly new and mature thirty-year-old outlook, I didn't buy anything.

That night I had a party at a bar. Close friends and acquaintances came to have a drink and wish me a happy thirtieth. Owen came with his fiancée, Jennifer with her husband. All of my newly divorced friends were there, single, as was I. Jeff sent me a happy birthday text. I didn't drink much at my party and was exhausted by all the events of the past six months. I allowed myself to be exhausted, said good-bye to my friends who were still there, and went home. I had a lovely time, but the whole thing was extremely anticlimactic. I was in bed by midnight.

A couple of days after my 1996 train accident, the *Providence Journal* printed a story about my attempt to jump onto a moving Amtrak train. It wasn't until reading the article that I learned the shocking truth. My train was not leaving the station at all. It was just pulling into the station. I wasn't late; the train was. That's why that Amtrak employee yelled, "Don't jump." Not because it was absurdly dangerous, but because he knew that had I waited a few more minutes for the train to come to a grinding stop, I could have stepped on, sat down, and returned to Boston safely, purple pens perpendicularly ready for class the next morning. But had I waited, I would never have had the unique experience of getting dragged under a train. I wouldn't have known that when my time does come to die, there will again be a feeling of calm. Had I waited, I never would have felt that moment of nirvana, known to trust in my survival instinct, or discovered the Playboy Channel.

From the middle, a train that is coming looks eerily similar to one that is going, like a relationship that is dying or growing. It's hard to tell upon first glance what is really happening. Yes, if I had waited a minute, been less impulsive, and been a bit more self-aware, I would not have married Jeff. But then where would I be? There is no way to know. But I do know, had I not married Jeff, I would never have learned all the things I needed to learn to one day have a healthy marriage. I never would have had a reason to look at myself so closely and to realize that I had been hiding behind his walls of pot smoke when I have walls of my own to break down. That I need to love myself before I can love anyone else, or allow anyone else to really love me. Had I not experienced a starter marriage I wouldn't have taken stock in what kind of relationships I am drawn to and why, and what my coping mechanisms are when I feel out of control. And I wouldn't have learned how to roll a cigarette or that the Cubs were cursed by a goat or that I love mint chocolate chip ice cream.

The night of my thirtieth birthday I fell asleep alone knowing there were a million things I needed to figure out. But I also fell asleep knowing I would never again be unhappy on someone else's terms. I would only be unhappy on my own terms. With that thought, I slept soundly.

Epilogue

Say Something Shocking at Your Mother's Seventieth Birthday Party

Susan, who acted like a sixteen-year-old and looked like a fifty-five-year-old, was turning seventy. After hundreds of edits of guest lists, many discussions about tablecloths, and nearly a year of planning, John threw her a big birthday party on a yacht that slowly circled around her hometown, New York City. Chauncey, Berns, and I were there along with sixty of her closest friends. That night was a culmination of a week of smaller parties, brunches, and events. During an especially touching moment, when one of Susan's oldest friends presented her with a book of pictures we had all painstakingly picked out, Susan started to blow her nose. She kept blowing her nose as she flipped through the past seventy years of her life. She looked up and said, "I've trained myself to cry out of my nose."

After her custom-made three-tiered crossword-puzzle cake was brought out, it was time for speeches. I had always been the designated speech giver of the three kids and it was my job to say a little something before giving the floor over to John. After a year of postdivorce therapy and a lot of soul-searching, I had decided months before exactly what I was going to say. Just because our family had always been one way didn't mean it always had to stay that way and maybe instead of following Susan's cues, I would write my own dialogue and she could follow mine.

I stood in front of the group, Susan to one side of me, and felt my heart pounding. I wasn't nervous about speaking but about what I was going to say.

"Millions of mothers are called Mom. Fewer are called Susan. But only one can claim she laughed when she saw a fishhook sticking out of her young son's eye, woke up one daughter in the middle of the night to watch *Eraserhead*, advised the other to always have a valid passport in case of necessary immediate fleeing of the country, gave her three hysterical children a brisk handshake after she almost drowned in the Colorado River, taught them a good vocabulary was more important than good manners, and advised that sex and drugs are fine as long as they don't end in prepositions. Shocking Susan was impossible because anything rebellious I did she had done more. But the one thing that has always rattled her is emotions. Especially sentimental ones. So I am going to say on her seventieth birthday, for the first time ever, the most shocking thing possible. Mom, I love you."

The group clapped and toasted as I put the mic down. I watched Susan's face. She didn't say "I love you" back but her nose was running, just a little. The next day as I was getting into an elevator to head to the airport for my flight back to L.A., Susan rushed over to me. She hugged me tightly and said, "I want you to know, I like you very much." It was a great start.

Author's Note

I've done my best to tell the truth, maybe even a little too much, and although the mind can easily morph memories, I have a lifelong supply of diaries to keep me honest. I admit to slight exaggeration at times and have changed a few details in order to protect the guilty. I have also changed most of the names in this memoir except for the names of my family members. When I found out I had a book deal I sent them this e-mail:

> This is extremely surreal, but I am starting to write the memoir. Can I use your real names? Let me know now or forever hold your outrage.
> xoxo
> S

These were their responses. . . .
From my father, John:

Author's Note

If you're the author, "Rothchild," and you're writing about your parents, what difference does it make if you disguise our names or not? Call me Sammy instead of John?

From my mother, Susan:

Only if you say nice things. You could call me Jessica.

From my sister, Berns:

Yeah, what the hell. XO Nerms

From my brother, Chauncey:

Well if Nerms is ok with it so am I, your sister Frankie.